ADVANCED
MASONRY

TIME
LIFE ®
BOOKS

Other Publications:

This volume is part of a series offering homeowners
detailed instructions on repairs, construction
and improvements they can undertake themselves.

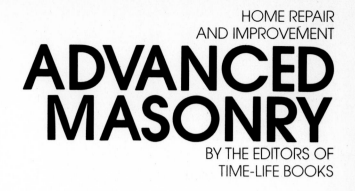

HOME REPAIR
AND IMPROVEMENT

ADVANCED MASONRY

BY THE EDITORS OF
TIME-LIFE BOOKS

TIME-LIFE BOOKS
ALEXANDRIA, VIRGINIA

THE CONSULTANTS: James Ailles, a professional mason since 1955, has worked on the construction of more than 100 major buildings, including a number of churches throughout North and South America.

Roswell W. Ard is a consulting structural engineer and a professional home inspector in northern Michigan. He has written professionally on construction techniques.

Harris Mitchell, special consultant for Canada, has worked in the field of home repair and improvement since 1950. He is Homes editor of *Today* magazine, writes a syndicated newspaper column, "You Wanted to Know," and is the author of a number of books on home improvement.

Cliff Stretmater is a structural engineer and general contractor in the Washington, D.C., metropolitan area. He has worked in design since 1959.

For information about any Time-Life book, please write:
Reader Information
Time-Life Books
541 North Fairbanks Court
Chicago, Illinois 60611

Library of Congress Cataloguing in Publication Data
Main entry under title:
Advanced masonry.
   (Home repair and improvement; 32)
   1. Masonry.   I. Time-Life Books.   II. Series.
TH5311.A27   693'.1   81-23241
ISBN 0-8094-3466-0   AACR2
ISBN 0-8094-3468-7 (on subscription)
ISBN 0-8094-3467-9 (lib. bdg.)

Contents

Mastering a Rugged Material

Masonry is a paradoxical material. Its chief properties—great strength and durability—make it both desirable and intimidating. On the positive side, brick, stone and concrete will not bend, corrode or rust as metal does; nor will they warp, rot or burn as wood does. Concrete has the advantage of assuming whatever form it is poured into; brick can be made in a wide range of shapes and sizes. Masonry structures do not have to be painted or sealed, and they require virtually no maintenance apart from an occasional cleaning.

Foremost among the intimidating traits of masonry is its weight. But this is mostly the result of viewing it in the mass. Although a finished brick wall does indeed exert hundreds of pounds of pressure on the footing beneath it, an individual brick weighs only 5 pounds—not a formidable measure. Concrete, with a weight of roughly 150 pounds per cubic foot, can nonetheless be rendered manageable either by reducing it to shovelful amounts or by having it poured directly into a waiting wheelbarrow, premixed, from the chute of a transit-mix truck.

In the great majority of situations, a thoughtful approach to the problem accomplishes more than muscle. For example, even a brick becomes heavy when held above shoulder height; but when worker and materials are elevated to the work level on a sturdy scaffold, little exertion is required.

Indeed, when dealing with masonry, the laws of physics are often more useful than a team of men. Archimedes claimed that, given the right place to stand—presumably somewhere in the heavens—he could move the earth with a lever. The mason uses the same principle to harvest stones, lifting them out of the ground with sturdy planks and a digging bar, or to dismantle a brick wall by means of a wrecking bar. And with the mechanical advantages of the pulley on a hoist standard, a single person can raise 200 pounds of material to the work platform of a sturdy scaffold.

Similarly, the problems posed by cutting and drilling into masonry can be overcome by means of the right tools and the right action. A brick will split cleanly in two with a gentle tap if the break line is first scored with a brickset. For heavy jobs, the use of a specialized power saw, much like a circular saw but larger and stronger, enables a worker to slice through a concrete block or lintel with relative ease. When it comes to drilling holes in concrete and stone, the key is to choose a power tool that augments the twisting action of a drill with the thrust of rapid pounding—a hammer drill or, for larger holes, a rotary hammer. Finally, there is an array of rugged hardware, designed specifically for masonry, that makes it easy to fasten almost anything to brick, stone, or concrete.

Bricks and Blocks for Plain and Fancy Walls

Unlike stones, which usually must be cut and then assembled like a jigsaw puzzle, bricks and blocks are made to fit together easily in regular patterns. In their most common modular forms, they are the basic materials of the mason's craft. But bricks and blocks can also be molded into a wide range of shapes that are suited to a variety of applications, from special structural functions to architectural detail. Brickyards often keep a few of the most widely used shapes in stock and can produce other special shapes to order.

Most wall construction calls for two types of brick: so-called building brick, the most economical, and face brick. Face bricks, available in many colors and surface textures, are used when uniform appearance or resistance to extreme weather conditions is required. The surface finish may appear on only one of the narrow sides, called the face.

A standard brick is nominally 8 inches long, 4 inches wide and ⅔ inches high—although its real dimensions are slightly less, to allow for mortar joints. These nominal dimensions are all based on even fractions of the brick's length. Thus, a brick is half as wide as it is long, and a third as high, permitting bricks to be laid in a variety of patterns while maintaining unbroken horizontal joints. Larger or smaller bricks are sometimes used for esthetic effect or to speed a job by using fewer bricks to fill a space. Specially shaped bricks are usually face bricks that conform to standard dimensions.

Bricks are available in three grades, based on their resistance to weathering. Bricks graded SW can withstand a high degree of frost action, as might occur in below-ground foundations or retaining walls. Grade MW bricks are used for less severe conditions, where frost is common but the bricks are unlikely to be permeated with water, as in an above-ground wall, for example. Grade NW applies only to building bricks and denotes minimal weather resistance. These bricks are used only for backup or interior walls. In Canada, where a different grading system is used, only Type 1 bricks are suitable for exposed faces.

If you order face bricks, be sure that they all come from the same batch; clay and manufacturing procedures may change from batch to batch, resulting in

A Myriad of Masonry Shapes

SOLID BRICK

FROGGED BRICK

CORED BRICK

COPING BRICK

OCTAGON BRICK

MOLDED BASE BRICK

ARCH BRICK

SILL BRICK

WATER-TABLE BRICK

Standard and custom bricks. Building bricks and face bricks are sold in one of three forms. There are solid bricks, which are flat on all sides. Frogged bricks, which also are solid, have a shallow depression—called a frog—on one of the two bed faces, which makes them lighter and allows stronger bonds. Cored bricks, the third kind, have holes cut all the way through them to reduce their weight.

Coping bricks provide an ornamental cap for a freestanding wall; ends and corners are finished with special matching units. Octagon bricks allow corners of 135°—the angle of an octagon; they come in two sizes to eliminate the need for cutting. Molded base bricks finish the base of a wall or column, or fill the angle of a wall stepped back to reduce its thickness. Although arches can be made with standard bricks, spe-

cial wedge-shaped bricks create a more regular appearance, allowing mortar joints of uniform thickness. Sill bricks create a slanting ledge under a window opening and come with special end bricks, with tablike extensions that are mortared into the adjoining brickwork. Water-table bricks are set 16 to 18 inches above the foundation; they divert the vertical flow of water outward, away from the foundation.

unacceptable variations in color and texture. If you are ordering special bricks as part of the job, they should be made and fired from the same batch of clay as the standard bricks in your order.

Bricks also vary in water absorption from batch to batch and should be tested before they are laid. Bricks that are too dry may draw water from fresh mortar, preventing the formation of a sound joint. Test a brick from each batch by sprinkling a few drops of water on its broad surface, called the bed. If the water is completely absorbed in less than one minute, hose down the entire batch. Then allow the surface water to be absorbed before laying the bricks.

The smallest number of standard bricks you can buy economically is a strap—100 bricks bound together by a metal band. Less expensive is a cube, or 500 bricks. Special bricks are usually sold in smaller quantities. Have the straps or cubes delivered on wooden pallets; otherwise they may be unloaded into a jumbled pile, with attendant breakage.

Concrete blocks are manufactured in fewer forms than bricks. The major variable is the aggregate mixed with cement to make the concrete. Standard blocks are made with sand, gravel and crushed stone; they weigh between 40 and 50 pounds and are used for applications where structural strength is required—bearing walls, for example. Lightweight blocks, also called cinder blocks, contain cinders, pumice or other light material instead of stone, and weigh between 25 and 35 pounds. They are not as strong as standard blocks and should be used only for nonbearing walls or light construction, where permitted by building codes.

Like bricks, blocks come in a standard size used in most construction; the nominal dimensions are 16 inches long, 8 inches wide and 8 inches high. Widths from 4 to 12 inches are available to meet varying specifications for strength or wall thickness. Specially shaped blocks can be ordered in dimensions conforming to those of standard blocks.

Many of the specially shaped concrete blocks are made for specific structural applications, such as tops and corners of walls. There also are ornamental blocks that relieve the visual monotony of a flat wall with texture, highlights and shadows, or rounded corners. If you use ornamental blocks in structural walls, be sure they are made with the proper aggregate.

Concrete blocks are usually delivered on wooden pallets, 48 blocks to the pallet. Unless otherwise specified, each pallet usually contains a mixture of stretcher and corner blocks in the proportions required for most ordinary structures.

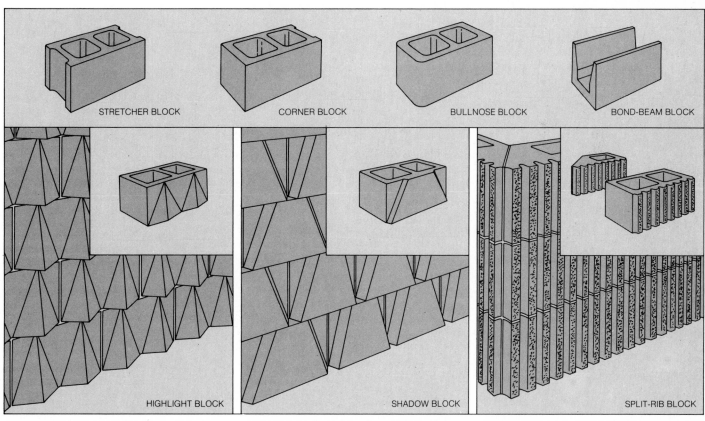

STRETCHER BLOCK   CORNER BLOCK   BULLNOSE BLOCK   BOND-BEAM BLOCK

HIGHLIGHT BLOCK   SHADOW BLOCK   SPLIT-RIB BLOCK

Standard and custom blocks. Most concrete-block walls are constructed with the four blocks shown above, all of them variants of the standard hollow block. Stretcher blocks, with flanges at each end, are used for long runs of wall where both ends are mortared to adjacent blocks. Corner blocks have one flat end for smooth surfaces at corners and wall ends; bullnose blocks, for similar applications, have one or two rounded corners. Channel-shaped bond-beam blocks—also known as speed blocks—are used to produce a continuous cavity along the top of a wall, which is filled with horizontal steel reinforcing rods and mortar.

Faceted blocks are examples of special faces designed to create an interplay of light and shadow when they are used in the construction of a wall. Split-rib blocks create an array of narrow vertical columns, which can be continued around a corner with the use of special matching blocks that have a mitered edge.

Selecting and Shaping Stone to Meet Your Needs

Stone, as a building material, has a lot to recommend it. The existence of stone buildings many centuries old attests to its strength and durability. Less evident is the fact that the cutting and shaping of stone are relatively simple tasks. Only a few hand tools are needed to fashion this widely available raw material into building blocks and to dress the surfaces to a smooth finish.

Though stone used for construction displays a vast array of colors and textures, most of it falls into a half dozen major types (chart, opposite). In choosing among them, two factors are paramount: structural strength and workability. A coarse-grained sandstone will crumble, for instance, if it is used for a load-bearing pier or in a wet, exposed location. Dense granite and limestone are suitably sturdy for almost any application, but they can be difficult to split. In fact, if you are planning to cut a great deal of stone into thin slabs for paving or veneer, look for stone that is marked by parallel striations, called the grain; these are natural break lines that will make splitting easier.

Stone for building comes in two basic forms—as fieldstone or as quarried stone. "Fieldstone" is a general term describing stones that have broken away from underlying bedrock through natural causes; they tend to be rounded and weathered. Fieldstone can be bought from building-materials suppliers or it can be dug out of the ground (page 15).

Quarried stone, cut or blasted from bedrock, has a fresh-cut appearance and sharper edges. Because it usually retains much of its ground-water content, called quarry sap, it is also easier to cut and shape, and its clean, unweathered surface bonds well with mortar. Quarried stone is available in a wide range of shapes and sizes, from fine gravel to pieces weighing hundreds of pounds. In construction sizes, most kinds of stone are available as flat pieces or as irregularly shaped rubble. Flat stones, up to 4 inches thick, are used for veneering, paving and laying coursed walls. Rubble, in diameters from 6 to 18 inches, is used for hearths, piers, and both mortared and un-mortared—"dry"—walls.

Beyond the immediate concerns for strength and workability, your choice of stone is likely to be governed by cost. Stone available through building-materials suppliers, as well as the marble and polished granite sold by monument masons, is often brought from distant sources. This adds appreciably to its cost: Because of its great weight, stone is expensive to transport. For this reason, local stone is generally cheaper. In addition, it tends to blend more harmoniously into its surroundings.

If one type of building stone is unusually prevalent in an area, chances are that a nearby quarry is supplying it. Most quarries will deliver stone directly to the building site, selling it by the cubic foot if it is rubble, by the square foot if it is flat stone. You can cut costs substantially by hauling the stone yourself in a rented truck or trailer. Some quarries will allow you to select the stone, enabling you to reject unsuitable sizes and shapes.

Even hand-picked stones, however, are unlikely to fit perfectly into every space in your project. And some projects require specially shaped stones, such as square-cut pieces, called quoins, for corners, or angled keystones for arches. These can be cut from larger stones and dressed to the desired shape. For jobs requiring paving or veneering, it will be necessary to split thick flat stones into thinner pieces.

Shaping stone is above all a gradual process: Impatience can reduce a usable stone to worthless scrap. Study each stone to determine its grain, evidenced by parallel layers or cracks, and plan to capitalize on this direction of natural splitting. Cutting across the grain is more difficult; except where cross-grain cracks are already present, you may get unwanted breaks. If the stone has no natural grain, its cutting characteristics will be the same in any direction, affected only by the density of the stone. In general, a dense stone such as granite requires many chipping blows before an irregular biock is turned into a square quoin; far fewer blows are needed to achieve a similar shape in slate or in sandstone, which are less dense.

The mason's basic shaping tool is a special hammer with a head that is blunt at one end and wedge-shaped at the other. Available in sizes ranging from 1½ to 8 pounds (the best weight for general use is 3 pounds), the stone hammer is used for breaking and splitting large stones or for chipping edges. Another hammer, called a maul, is blunt at both ends. It is used to strike chisels in dressing the face of a stone and to drive the wedge-shaped end of the stone hammer into stubborn splits. A 3-pound maul will handle most jobs. Also useful for quick, fine shaping of soft stones is a bricklayer's hammer with a chipping blade.

A basic set of chisels to use with the maul should include a wide-bladed stone chisel for splitting, cutting and notching stone; a sharp-tipped pointing tool for fine dressing; and several widths of cold chisels, which masons called pitching tools, for shearing off small protrusions.

Small stones can be hand-held during the shaping process, but heavier pieces should be placed on a low, sturdy workbench or on the ground. The bench or ground should be cushioned with rubber pads, sand, sawdust or several layers of carpet to absorb the force of the cutting blow. Lack of cushioning may cause the stone to break at the point where it touches the work surface rather than on the face being struck.

Finally, whenever you are cutting or dressing stone, wear leather gloves and protective goggles to guard against injury from jagged edges and flying shards.

A Guide to Common Building Stones

Type	Weight	Durability	Water resistance	Workability	Color	Texture	Uses
Granite	Heavy	Good	Good	Difficult	Various grays	Fine to coarse	Building
Basalt	Heavy	Excellent	Excellent	Difficult	Black	Fine	Paving
Limestone	Heavy	Fair	Poor	Medium to difficult	Various	Fine to coarse	Building, veneering
Slate	Medium	Good	Excellent	Easy	Purple, gray, green	Fine	Veneering, paving
Shale	Medium	Poor	Poor	Easy	Various	Fine	Veneering
Sandstone	Light to medium	Fair	Fair	Easy to medium	Various	Fine to coarse	Building, veneering

Choosing stone. This chart shows relative weights and other properties of the basic stone types used in construction. It is only a general guide; stones in each type can vary greatly, depending on the region where they are found.

Splitting Stone into Flat Slabs

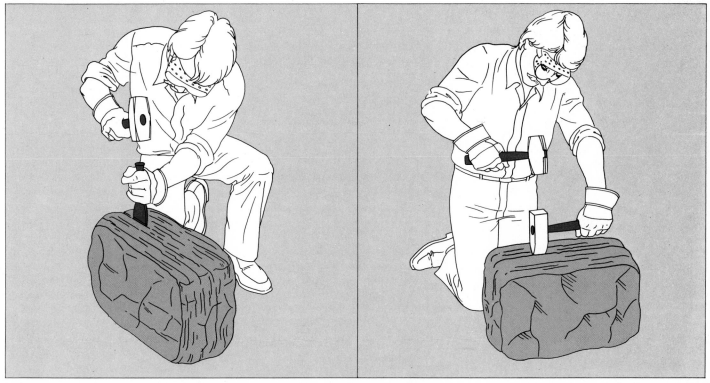

Chiseling with the grain. Incise the splitting line on one long face of the stone with a wide-bladed stone chisel, lightly tapping the chisel with a maul *(above, left)*. When you have marked the entire line, return to the starting point and strike the chisel with more force, once again traversing the line. Repeat until the stone splits.

If the stone cracks but does not split, you will have to use a stone hammer: Align its wedge-shaped end with the crack *(above, right)*, then strike the flat face of the hammer firmly with the maul. Move the stone hammer little by little along the crack you have made, striking it repeatedly until the stone splits apart.

Squaring the Faces
of a Corner Stone

1 Rough-chipping a flat face. Scribe the cutting line on the stone with the corner of a stone chisel, and lay the stone on the ground, waste edge facing you. Chip off small pieces from the waste edge by striking the stone glancing blows with the blunt end of the stone hammer; hold the hammer at a slight angle so that only the edge of the hammer face strikes the stone. Continue chipping until you have reduced most of the surface unevenness and are within ½ inch of the cutting line. Check the work occasionally with a try square to be sure the new face is perpendicular to the adjoining faces of the stone.

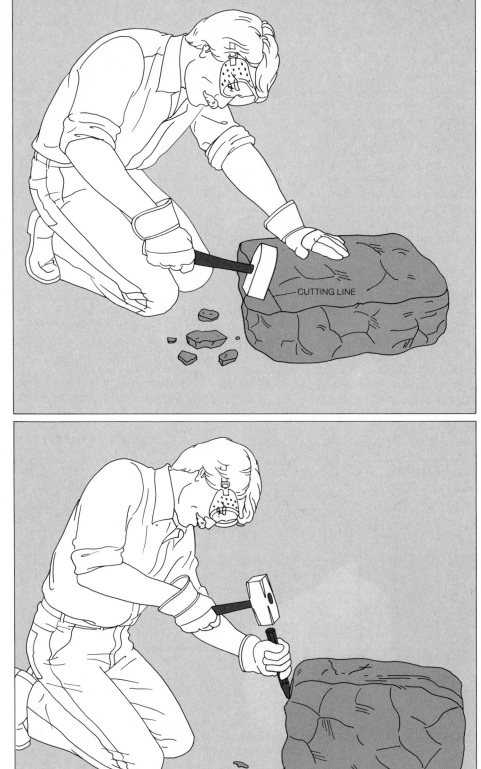

CUTTING LINE

2 Pitching the flattened face. Turn the stone on end and, using a 1-inch pitching tool with a 3-pound maul, chisel away the remaining waste edge. Hold the chisel at about a 30° angle to the face of the stone, and work from the ends toward the center, cutting a little at a time and turning the stone as required. When only small protrusions remain, remove them with a pointing tool, using the same chiseling technique.

Breaking across a Stone's Grain

1 **Cutting a groove.** Working on the ground or on a cushioned workbench, cut a shallow groove across one face of the stone with a wide-bladed stone chisel and a maul. Hold the chisel so that only a corner of its blade contacts the stone, and tap it lightly. Repeat this cut, each time tapping the chisel more firmly, until the depth of the groove is about one fifth of the stone's thickness. Turn the stone over and groove the other face in the same way, lining up the grooves as accurately as possible. Then groove each edge so that the stone is completely girdled.

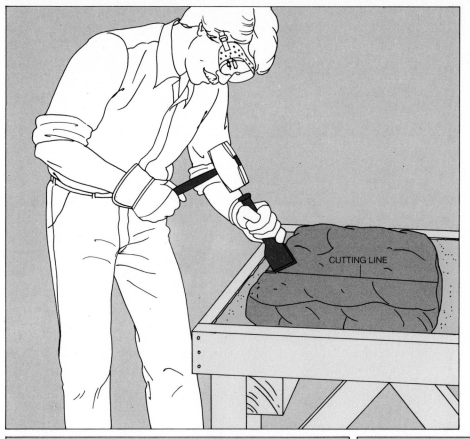

CUTTING LINE

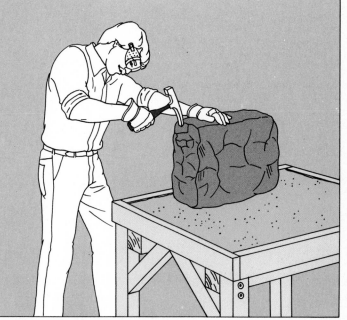

2 **Snapping off the waste.** Align the groove with the edge of the workbench or a sturdy board, and strike the overhanging waste edge with a stone hammer. Bring the hammer down sharply, full face against the surface of the stone. If necessary, press down on the other edge of the stone with your free hand, so that the stone will not flip up from the force of the blow.

3 **Dressing the cut edge.** Stand the stone upright, cut edge facing you, and chip away small uneven parts with the chisel end of a bricklayer's hammer. Work toward the center of the stone, and strike across the base of each protrusion, in effect lifting it from the surface of the stone. To remove any large protrusions, use a pitching tool and a maul, as shown in Step 2, opposite.

Chipping Stone into a Curve

1 Scoring the curve. Make a template of heavy cardboard cut to the desired curve and, using it as a guide, scratch a cutting line on the face of the stone with the corner of a wide-bladed stone chisel. Mark the opposite face of the stone in the same manner, aligning the template with the first cutting line at the edges of the stone. Then score grooves along both of these lines, using a wide-bladed stone chisel and a maul, as described in Step 1, page 13.

2 Removing the waste. Working along the edge of the waste, chip out large flakes, about half the thickness of the stone, using the chisel end of a bricklayer's hammer. When the entire edge has been undercut, or thinned, tap the flat side of the edge with a stone hammer, to snap it off. Then undercut the new edge of the waste in the same way, continuing to remove the stone in flakes until you reach the scored groove defining the curve. Then dress, or finish, the curved edge with a pitching tool and a pointing tool as described in Step 2, page 12.

CARDBOARD TEMPLATE

Salvaging Rocks Acquired Free

If you have access to rocky land or a stony creek, you may be able to gather the stone for a project at no cost—not, at least, for the stone. Farmers are often happy to be rid of stones plowed from their fields, and the verges of newly graded roads frequently abound in stones unearthed by bulldozers. Abandoned mines and quarries, shown on geological survey maps, may be surrounded by tailings rich in usable stones. And ruined stone chimneys, foundations and walls contain stones of proven utility.

Check with the property owner before collecting such free stone; it may have been earmarked for another use, or it may have esthetic or historical value.

Because of the sheer weight involved—one cubic foot of granite may weigh 175 pounds—gathering stone calls for some special procedures. If you must transport the stone over a long distance, rent a truck or trailer designed for heavy loads, and do not overload the vehicle, which would make it difficult to steer. Distribute the stones evenly, and pile partial loads toward the front of the bed.

In preparing to load the stones, drive as close to them as possible. Use a sturdy wheelbarrow to move them to the truck; you will need a helper to lift most large stones. If the terrain is very rough, you may have to make a heavy sled, or stone boat. It should be built of 2-inch lumber, with removable sides and with runners on the bottom, capped with flat steel bars if possible. It must be low enough to allow stones to be tumbled rather than lifted onto it, and it should have a chain or heavy rope at each end, to use for pulling the sled or for lowering it down steep slopes.

The best tool for stone gathering is a 30-pound 60-inch pry bar or digging bar, available at building-supply houses. It functions primarily as a lever for prying stones from the earth or a wall, or for tipping them onto the stone boat. It can also be used to split large stones.

A fresh cache of fieldstones may hide insects, rodents or snakes. Heavy leather gloves can protect your hands from bites and stings as well as from the jagged edges of the stones.

Excavating a Large Fieldstone

1 **Digging out a stone.** With a pick and a shovel, dig a trench around the stone deep enough that you can slip a 5-foot digging bar under it. Leave a pile of earth beside the trench; top it with a sturdy flat rock to act as a fulcrum for the bar. Push down on the outer end of the bar to free the stone, while a helper slips a rock beneath the stone to support it. Repeat the levering process on the other side until the stone is completely free and rests on its rock supports. Then slide two long, sturdy 2-by-6 planks as far as possible under the stone.

2 **Working the stone out of the hole.** Using the 2-by-6 planks as levers and the digging bar as a prod, lift the stone out of the hole. First work the stone onto the planks by prying and pushing with the digging bar, keeping the planks close together to support the stone. Then, bracing the stone with the bar to prevent it from rolling back into the hole, have your helper push down on the outer ends of the planks to lift the stone to ground level. Now slide the bar across the hole, under both planks, to support them, while your helper rolls the stone along the planks and onto the stone boat. When the stone is partway on the boat, pull the bar from under the planks and use it to lever the stone all the way onto the boat.

Drilling and Cutting Through Masonry

Cutting through concrete and drilling holes in brick are not exactly easy tasks, but a number of special tools are available to help cope with the challenge. The simplest tool for making a hole is a star drill, a pointed four-bladed chisel. Used with a small sledge hammer called a maul, a star drill can make holes larger than an inch in diameter. Unfortunately, the holes often have ragged edges, so the tool is best used where the final appearance is of little importance.

To make clean small-bore holes such as those needed to seat masonry fasteners *(page 20)*, choose an electric hammer drill equipped with a carbide-tipped bit. Designed to drill holes less than 1 inch in diameter, it combines the twisting action of a regular electric drill with the rapid, repeated thrust of a trip hammer—50,000 times per minute on some models. Moreover, if the job demands drilling a matching hole in wood, the hammer action can be eliminated. Small-bore holes can also be drilled in masonry with a standard electric drill fitted with a carbide-tipped bit, but the work will be much slower.

For smooth-bore holes larger than 1 inch in diameter, the best tool is a rotary hammer, a larger and noisier version of the hammer drill. A rotary hammer also combines drilling and hammering, but it can weigh three times as much as a hammer drill, and it will drive a bit into masonry with tremendous force. It can bore 3½-inch holes in solid concrete.

Depending on the needs of the job, the rotary hammer can be switched from the combination drill-and-hammer action to a DRILL ONLY or a HAMMER ONLY mode. When set to HAMMER ONLY, a rotary hammer can be fitted with special-purpose chisel bits and can be used as a hand-held jackhammer to blast sizable openings in masonry walls. For instance, a rotary hammer can make a hole in a concrete foundation wall large enough for a clothes-dryer vent *(page 18)*.

For sawing through heavy masonry such as concrete blocks and lintels, the ideal tool is an abrasive saw. Similar to a circular saw fitted with a masonry blade, the abrasive saw applies more power and uses a larger blade. Like a regular mason-ry blade, the blade of an abrasive saw consists of hard silica grits, glued together. The grits wear down during use, so the blade must be replaced periodically.

To avoid injury when using any of these tools, certain safety precautions must be strictly observed. Always unplug electric tools before adjusting them or changing their bits or blades. Wear goggles at all times; even a star drill is likely to spray sharp bits of masonry as it cuts. With power tools, you should also wear a respirator to filter dust from the air. Sturdy work gloves are essential, to protect your hands from flying particles and also to provide a cushion against vibrations.

An abrasive saw poses an additional danger. If its blade has been dropped or develops an invisible crack, it could fly apart in use. Test a suspect blade by suspending it on a pencil and tapping it with a screwdriver handle—if it rings with a sharp bell tone, the blade is good.

Lastly, when you are using any power tool, be sure to keep the work area clear of rubble and dust so that you do not slip and lose your balance.

A Hand-Held Drill for Rough-Cut Holes

Cutting a hole with a star drill. Place the point of the star drill on the spot marking the center of the hole you want to bore. Hold the drill perpendicular to the wall and rap it smartly with a maul. Rotate the drill slightly after each hammer blow to prevent the four cutting blades from getting stuck in the masonry. Go on hammering and rotating the drill until the hole is deep enough. After the hole is finished, clear it of dust and debris with a blowout bulb *(inset)*.

BLOWOUT BULB

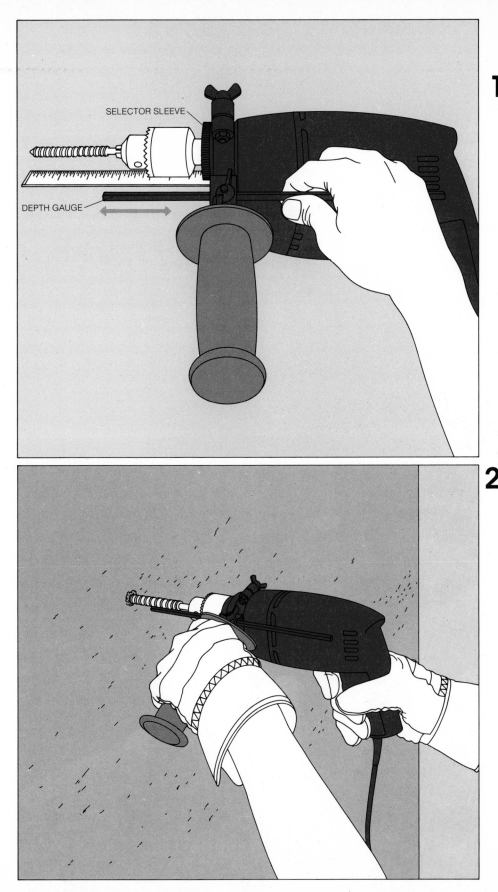

A Percussive Drill
for Boring Small Holes

1 **Preparing the drill.** With the cord un-plugged, fit a bit of the required diameter into the drill; use a bit at least 1 inch longer than the desired depth of the hole. Lay the drill on a flat surface and loosen the wing nut that se-cures the depth gauge. Place a ruler under the bit, aligning the end of the ruler with the tip of the bit. Slide the depth gauge forward or backward until the end of the gauge lines up with the mark on the ruler corresponding to the desired depth of the hole. Tighten the wing nut to secure the gauge.

If the hammer drill has no depth gauge, mark the desired depth of the hole directly on the bit. Wrap the bit with tape at the point where you want the drilling to stop.

To set the hammer-drill function, rotate the arrow on the selector sleeve—located just be-hind the chuck—to HAMMER DRILL or DRILL.

SELECTOR SLEEVE

DEPTH GAUGE

2 **Boring masonry with a hammer drill.** Mark the center of the desired hole. Touch the point of the bit to the mark, then turn on the ham-mer drill, and press it forward. Use just enough pressure to keep the bit in contact with the masonry. Drill to the desired depth.

The Repertoire of a Rotary Hammer

Chiseling through concrete. Mark the outline of the proposed opening, and notch a starter hole in its center with a star drill. Set the rotary hammer for HAMMER ONLY and attach a bull-point chisel bit, following the instructions appropriate to the model. Grip the hammer firmly in both hands and touch the bit to the starter hole. Turn on the hammer, and drill straight into the starter hole. After you have penetrated about 4 inches, turn off the hammer, withdraw the bit and reposition it at the edge of the hole; then turn on the hammer again and widen the cut. Continue in this manner until you reach the outline. Then rework the cut area, deepening it until you pierce the concrete. Rest the hammer occasionally to prevent it from overheating.

Removing unwanted mortar. Fitted with various specialized bits, the rotary hammer speeds cleanup tasks; always set the tool for HAMMER ONLY. Use the scaling chisel *(top right)* to scrape off spattered mortar; hold the tool almost parallel to the wall so that the bit lifts off the debris without gouging the surface.

The pointed mortar-cutting chisel *(middle right)* is used to chip out crumbling mortar from joints that are to be tuck pointed. Break up the mortar with the pointed tip, then use the wider blade edge to cut out whatever the tip does not dislodge. Use the serrated blade of the slotting chisel *(bottom right)* to cut a neat, narrow slot into a mortar joint. With this bit you can remove one or more bricks from a wall.

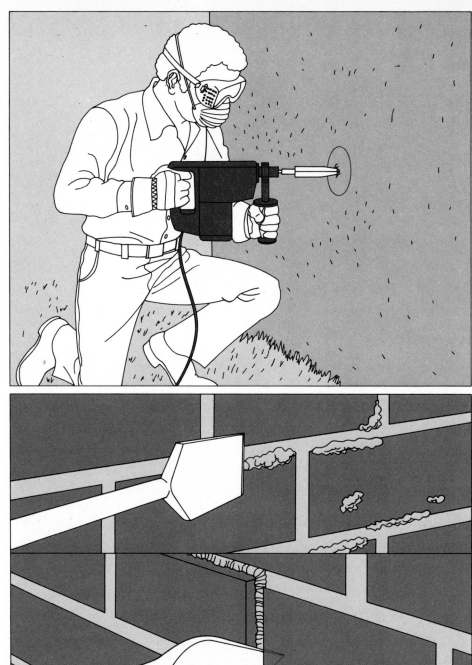

GUIDE FRAME

A Saw That Slices Through Concrete Block

Adjusting the depth of cut. With the saw unplugged, locate and loosen the nuts that hold the guide frame in place. Tilt the saw on its side, and adjust the guide frame until the distance between the frame and the bottom of the blade equals the desired depth. Tighten the nuts again to secure the guide frame.

Operating the saw. Using pencil or a marking crayon, outline the desired opening on the concrete-block wall—in this example, a rectangular niche for a steel girder. Wherever possible, allow the outline to follow mortar joints. Set the guide frame so that the initial cut will be ½ inch deep; position the blade over the cutting line, about 6 inches in from one corner of the rectangle. Turn on the saw and lower the blade onto the line, holding it there until the guide frame touches the masonry. Then move the saw forward until the leading edge of the blade reaches the next corner. Turn off the saw and lift it from the cut. Following the same procedure, make identical cuts on the other three sides of the rectangle.

Reset the guide frame to cut 1 inch deeper, and retrace the original cut. Repeat until you have reached the desired depth—or until you have cut as deep as the saw will go, usually 4½ inches. Use a cold chisel and a maul to complete the cut at the corners, where the blade penetrated less deeply, then break up the blocks within the outline and remove them.

Nails and Bolts for Piercing Masonry Surfaces

Things mounted to masonry—furring strips, electrical outlets, basketball backboards, stair-rail balusters—call for fastening hardware rugged enough to penetrate rock-hard materials and grip tightly. Fortunately, the choice is wide *(chart, opposite),* largely because industry, a prime user of fasteners, has spawned a variety of solutions for particular fastening jobs. In making a choice among them, you must consider both the load on the fastener and the composition of the masonry itself.

For almost every fastening job there are several fasteners that will fit the bill. The simplest of these are inserted directly into the masonry: nails, pins and screws. Masonry nails, made of hardened steel, can be driven with a heavy hammer, such as a hand sledge, a blacksmith's hammer or a ball-peen hammer. Accessories for hammering nails into masonry include magnetic punches, or nail starters *(below, left),* for steadying the work in tight places and, for safety, a pair of shatterproof safety goggles.

Steel pins, which are a bit lighter than nails but are longer and are designed to penetrate the masonry more deeply, have to be driven with a stud driver. This tool consists of a protective barrel, which holds the pin, and a piston, which fits into the barrel and rams the pin into the masonry. For small jobs, a manual stud driver, used with a hammer, serves well enough *(below, right);* but if you are going to have many pins to drive, it may be best to rent a power stud driver. This tool—which is literally a kind of gun—uses the explosive force of a .22-caliber blank to drive the piston against the pin.

Although a power stud driver is reasonably safe when handled with care, its operation may vary from one model to another. Be sure that you get the manufacturer's instructions for the exact model you are renting, and have the clerk at the rental agency check you out on the tool before you take it home.

The masonry screw, the third type of fastener that is made to be inserted directly into masonry, is often used in situations where hammering could ruin the appearance of a masonry surface. The screw is driven into a pilot hole; in the process, its specially designed notched threads cut a spiral groove. To ensure that the hole will be exactly the right size, most manufacturers supply a drill bit with each box of screws.

Although nails, pins and screws serve for most jobs, they have their limitations. In soft masonry they provide only light holding power, and they are difficult to drive into hard masonry such as granite or old, dense concrete, which over the years will have cured rock-hard. For these surfaces, as well as for mounting heavy loads on brick or standard concrete, you will need the added holding power of a two-part fastening system.

Typically, this consists of a bolt or screw, and a sleeve—or expansion anchor—of metal, plastic or fiber. The expansion anchor is inserted into a drilled hole *(pages 16-18),* and the fastener is then driven into the anchor, expanding it to grip the hole and wedge the assembly in place. A second type of anchor, called a toggle, is used in hollow walls; it consists of a screw or a bolt fitted with a pair of retractable wings that open and grip the inside wall surface when the screw or bolt is tightened.

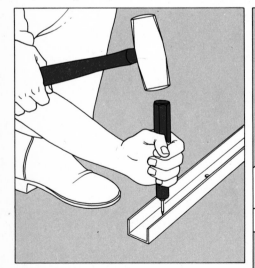

Nailing in close quarters. Center the head of a masonry nail on the circular, magnetized end of a nail starter; position the nail against the object being mounted—in this case, a channel for a porch-enclosure panel. Tap the hexagonal end lightly with a small sledge hammer or a heavy ball-peen hammer to break the masonry surface. Then drive the nail home with heavier blows.

Setting a steel pin. Slip the head of a pin into the barrel of a stud driver *(above, left),* pushing the pin until the metal washer behind its point touches the end of the barrel. Press the point of the pin against the object being mounted on the masonry—in this example, a furring strip

(above, right). Grasp the handgrip firmly and rap the driver piston sharply with a heavy hammer, which will force the pin through the washer and into the masonry. When the steel pin is fully set, the washer will prevent the fixture from working its way loose.

Suiting the Fastening to the Surface and the Load

Type of fastener		Installation method	Adobe	Block, hollow part	Block, solid part	Brick	Concrete, dense	Concrete, standard	Mortar joints	Stone, hard	Stone, soft
Masonry nail		Choose a nail that will penetrate masonry ½ to ¾ inch. Tap lightly to start; then pound home with heavier blows.			○	○	●	●	○	●	○
Steel pin		Drive by hand with a stud driver (*opposite*), or rent a .22-caliber power driver; operate according to instructions.			○	○	●	●	○	○	○
Masonry screw		Drill hole with bit supplied with the screws. Drive screw through object being mounted, into hole.	○		○	○	●	○	○		
Plastic nail anchor		Drill hole the diameter of anchor. Position object, insert anchor through it and drive nail into hole.	○	○	○	○	○	○	○	○	○
Plastic screw anchor		Drill hole the diameter of anchor. Tap anchor into hole until top is flush with surface; position object and drive screw.	○	○	○	○	○	○	○	○	○
Fiber screw anchor		Drill hole slightly larger than anchor. Push anchor into hole; position object and drive screw.	○	○	●	●	●	●	○	●	○
Metal nail anchor		Drill hole the diameter of anchor. Position object, insert anchor; tap lightly to seat, then drive nail with sharp blows.		○	●	●	●	●	●	●	○
Lag shield		Drill hole, insert shield, position object, and drive lag screw. In mortar joints, set shield so that it expands against the masonry units.	○		●	●	●	●	●	●	○
Expansion stud		Drill hole the diameter of anchor through object and into masonry. Insert screw or bolt into anchor, tap into hole and tighten.	●		●	●	●	●	●	●	●
Hammer-set anchor		Drill hole the diameter of anchor. Fill hole with one or more anchors. Tap with hammer and pipe or setting tool to seat; insert bolt and tighten.			●	●	●	●	●	●	●
Plastic toggle		Drill ⁵⁄₁₆-inch hole. Flatten anchor and push into hole. Position object, insert screw and tighten.		○							
Metal toggle		Drill hole to fit folded toggle. Push bolt through object; add toggle. Insert toggle into hole, pull to hold against inside of wall and tighten.		●							

Picking an anchor. The left-hand column on the chart above shows the 12 most common kinds of masonry fasteners that are readily available for home use; the next column explains how each kind is installed. The nine narrow columns on the right-hand portion of the chart indicate the masonry surfaces for which each kind of fastener is appropriate and the degree of security that each one can provide. A solid dot in the col-umn means that the fastener or anchor is sturdy enough to withstand the pressures of virtually any kind of household structure—including book-shelves and stair handrails—provided the sur-rounding masonry is sound. An open circle in the column indicates that the fastener or anchor should be used for light loads only, such as small mirrors, boxes for electrical outlets or furring strips for mounting wallboard.

A Systematic Approach to Breaking Up Masonry

Dismantling masonry requires an artful combination of thoughtful planning and brute force. Every demolition project is really a problem in unbuilding and, like its counterpart, must begin with a careful assessment of the difficulty at hand.

Some projects should be immediately turned over to a professional: Load-bearing walls and walls of reinforced concrete to be demolished fall into this category. Removing a wall that abuts a bearing wall or a slab that adjoins a foundation may have structural implications, and an architect or an engineer should be consulted before demolition begins. And every project requires a call to the local building department to determine if it is covered by code. Thereafter, the choice of tools and the best way to use them depend on the type and condition of the masonry to be removed.

The basic procedure in any demolition project is to break up the masonry into manageable pieces. For a concrete slab or a tile patio, the simplest tool to use is a sledge hammer. But large stretches of sound masonry are more quickly demolished with an electric jackhammer, a tool similar to the pneumatic hammers used by road-mending crews except that this one runs on ordinary house current. With either tool, begin at the edge of the slab and work inward, so that the rubble can be easily removed as you proceed.

You can obtain an electric jackhammer from a tool-rental agency, along with a spikelike bull-point bit and a 3-inch chisel bit. At the same time assemble the necessary safety equipment: goggles, hearing protectors, and a respirator to block the plentiful dust raised by a jackhammer. Indoors, use a vapor-proof respirator, the kind worn in spray painting; outdoors, a dust mask is adequate.

For any demolition job, it makes sense to start at a weak point in the structure. In a masonry wall of brick, block or stone, that weak point is usually the mortar joints. Old, cracked or crumbling joints can often be pried open with a long pry bar, called a wrecking bar. But the sound joints of a newer wall must be dismantled more gradually, with a cold chisel and a maul. Since a masonry wall is strongest at its corners and its piers (page 98), dismantle it outward from the mid-dle of each panel and from the top down.

Because bricks are held in place by the force of the bricks around them, the first brick to be removed from each course of a wall will be the most difficult; it must often be smashed with the maul. Subsequent bricks can usually be pried out fairly easily. But for some modern walls, where the mortar joints are as strong as the bricks, you may need to do almost as much smashing as prying. In fact, if you do not plan to salvage bricks or if you are breaking up a concrete-block wall, you can use the smashing power of the maul to reduce the wall to rubble in no time. Whatever procedure you use, do not work above shoulder level. Use a stepladder or low scaffolding (page 24) to lift your head and shoulders safely above falling debris.

Demolishing a Concrete Slab

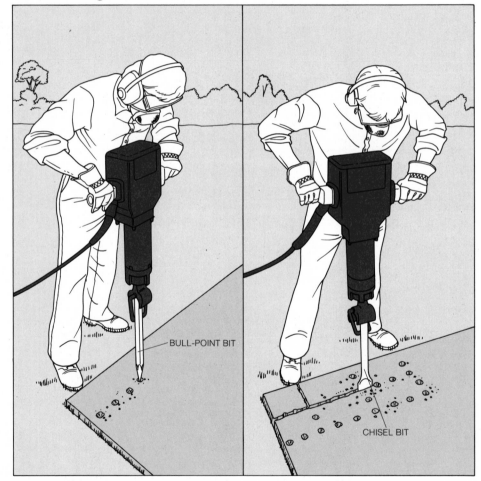

BULL-POINT BIT

CHISEL BIT

Using a jackhammer. With a bull-point bit, chop a row of holes 3 inches apart and 6 inches in from the slab edge (above, left). Then chop a parallel row of holes 6 inches in from the first. Connect these rows with similar rows, chopped at right angles to them and roughly 9 inches apart, creating a gridlike pattern. To make each hole, position the bit against the slab, then press the trigger on the hammer handle. Hold the hammer steady until the bit penetrates the full thickness of the slab. Stop the hammer, pull it from the hole and reposition it.

After drilling an area of roughly 3 square feet, set the 3-inch chisel bit in the hammer. Chop along the rows of holes (above, right) to break the slab into pieces. As you work, alternate periods of clearing rubble with periods of hammering. Because of the noise and vibration, never hammer for more than a half hour at a stretch.

Two Ways to Dismantle a Brick Wall

Loosening mortar with a cold chisel. Using a maul and wearing goggles to protect your eyes from flying fragments, pound the chisel deep into the vertical mortar joints at each end of a brick *(below, left)*. Sweep the mortar out with the chisel point. Then drive the chisel deep into the center of the horizontal joint below the brick. Angle the chisel downward into the joint at first; it will level out as it penetrates the joint. Then press down on the chisel to pry out the brick. If it does not pop out, break the brick with the maul and chisel it out in pieces, along with the surrounding mortar. Continue in this way, removing adjacent bricks *(below, right)* until the entire course is cleared.

HEADER COURSE

Prying out bricks with a wrecking bar. Wearing goggles to protect your eyes from mortar dust, force the angled end of the bar into a cracked or crumbling mortar joint. Using the bar as a lever, press down on its curved end to topple the section of wall above. If the wrecking bar does not dislodge the bricks, remove it and strike the wall with a sledge hammer to loosen the mortar joints. Direct the blows at the wall just above the point where you inserted the wrecking bar. Alternate the use of the wrecking bar and the sledge hammer until the wall topples.

If you are dismantling a double-thick wall that contains header courses interspersed with stretcher courses, try to pry up the header bricks; if you can do this, you will topple both thicknesses of brick above them.

Cleaning old bricks. Wearing goggles and gloves to protect your eyes and hands, chip the mortar from each brick with the blade of a bricklayer's hammer or slice along each face of the brick with a piece of flat steel such as a leaf spring or a tire iron, or the dulled blade of a hatchet. To clean bricks thoroughly, scrub them with a wire brush. Use a 1-to-10 solution of muriatic acid to remove all traces of mortar film; work outside, wearing goggles and rubber gloves.

How thoroughly you clean bricks depends on how you will reuse them. Bricks to be remortared must be flat but need not be entirely clean. Bricks to be laid flat in a patio must be free of mortar chunks, but mortar film will wear off under traffic and weather. Bricks that will not be exposed to wear and weather, as on an indoor hearth, may be cleaned with muriatic acid.

A Skeletal Frame for Scaling Heights

For many advanced masonry projects, the work involved is not more complex than simple masonry, but it is often more arduous, requiring the worker to lift and lay stone, brick or concrete block well above chest height. The way to make the work less onerous is to keep abreast of a rising wall by means of masonry scaffolding. The safest and fastest scaffolding to erect is made of tubular steel sections that couple and lock together quickly and easily. The most efficient working arrangement provides for two separate platforms: One is for stockpiling building materials; the other, a work platform, gives the worker a place to stand.

The materials platform ordinarily measures 5 by 7 feet and consists of three walk boards suspended side by side between the four legs of a scaffolding section. It will hold about 1,700 pounds. The work platform, a single walk board, clamps to the side of a scaffolding section, bringing the worker close to the rising wall. It is commonly about 2 feet wide and 7 feet long and should be capable of holding about 750 pounds.

The crucial requirement of any scaffolding is stability, which is achieved by adjusting the scaffolding to the existing terrain, by bracing it as it is assembled, and by loading it properly during use.

Before erecting the scaffolding, inspect the terrain for hazards, such as low-hanging power lines and soft backfill. If power lines threaten to interfere with the placement of the scaffolding, ask the local power company if service can be temporarily shut off. On any surface other than asphalt or concrete, stabilize the legs with 2-by-12 planks placed under the end frames and, if the ground also dips in places, place separate 2-by-12 base pads under individual legs.

On uneven terrain, perhaps the most commonly encountered problem, the placement of the first tier of scaffolding is crucial. Start by erecting a section at the highest point of ground. As you add sections to it, adjust the base plates on the legs to bring the sections level. Where the normal base-plate adjustment cannot compensate for the change in grade, add an extension leg.

When the scaffolding extends more than 30 feet and rises more than three stacked sections—or higher than 26 feet—it should be braced. If possible, the bracing should be anchored at the window openings, where it will not interfere with work in progress.

One bracing method uses two 2-by-4s, nailed together, to span the window openings. Heavy-gauge baling wire is then strung from the doubled 2-by-4s to a scaffolding end frame and twisted tight. A rope, tied to the opposite leg of the frame, leads to a stake in the ground that acts as a counterbrace. A second method employs a special metal brace, available as an accessory. It clamps to the scaffold and then is nailed or bolted to any stable structure, such as a stud or the mortar joint of an existing backup wall.

After the scaffold is in place, it is important to monitor the load, keep track of the weight and make sure it is evenly distributed. As a quick reference, the average brick weighs 4½ to 5 pounds; one hollow-core concrete block weighs between 25 and 35 pounds; and 1 cubic foot of mortar, with the mortar pan, weighs about 125 pounds. In calculating the total load, do not forget to add the weight of the workers on the scaffold. It is wise to keep the total load well below the manufacturer's weight limits.

Masonry scaffolding is readily available, along with accessories, from rental companies. Many of the suppliers will deliver the scaffolding to the job site and pick it up when the job is finished.

Stabilizing a Scaffold to Make It Safe

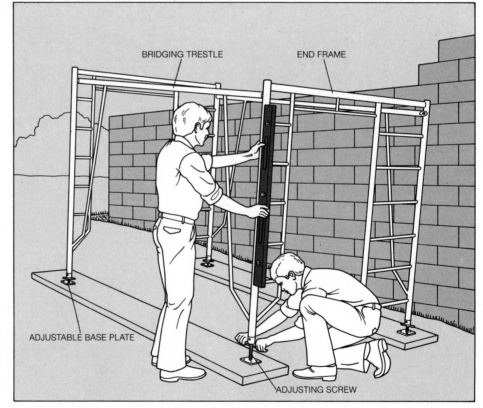

Leveling the base on sloping terrain. Assemble the first section of scaffolding by inserting adjustable base plates into the four legs. Position the assembly on the work site, with one end frame resting on the highest point of ground. Place two 2-by-12 planks lengthwise under the legs, linking the high and low end frames. Hold a mason's level against one leg of the low end frame while a helper adjusts the position of the base plate until the leg is plumb. Repeat this procedure at the other leg of the low end frame. Then hold the level across the top of this end frame to check it for horizontal alignment; readjust the legs as necessary. When the low end frame is level and plumb, check and adjust the high end frame for horizontal alignment.

Bracing a tall scaffold. When a scaffold rises more than 26 feet, tie it to the ground and to the wall surface with braces. To use a window opening for bracing, nail together two 2-by-4s, 8 inches longer than the window's width. Loop heavy-gauge baling wire over the 2-by-4s and wedge them behind the opening. Fasten the wire to the nearest end frame, twisting the ends together with pliers until the wire is taut.

Directly opposite the same end frame, drive a 2-by-6 stake, 4 feet long, into the ground; angle the stake slightly away from the scaffolding. Tie the end frame to the stake with a length of 1-inch-thick hemp or nylon rope. Then adjust the tension between the two points—the ground and the window brace—by inserting a short 2-by-3 between the strands of baling wire and twisting it until the rope at ground level is taut.

To use the metal brace sometimes supplied with scaffolding, clamp it to the end frame next to a window opening's jack stud, and nail it to the stud with a double-headed nail *(inset)*.

To attach a metal brace to a masonry backup wall, drill a hole into a mortar joint on the wall *(page 17)*, insert a lag shield, then drive an anchor bolt through the brace into the lag shield.

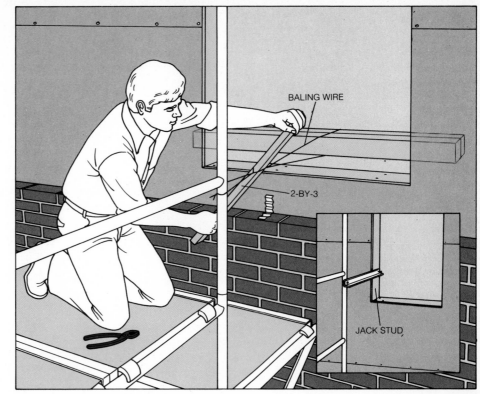

A Custom-built Structure

Anatomy of masonry scaffolding. The tubular-steel framework of scaffolding is made of interchangeable parts. Essential to its composition are two end frames, to which other parts are clamped. The end frames shown are a 6½-foot walk-through frame with built-in ladders, which allows work room under the scaffold, and a standard 4-foot mason's frame, whose horizontal rungs support a materials platform made from three aluminum-framed plywood walk boards. Side brackets extend 2 feet from the scaffold to support the work platform. Both platforms can be set up to keep the work and the materials at a convenient height.

The end-frame legs are stabilized by 2-by-12 wood planks, the sills; on uneven ground, individual 2-by-12 base pads are used instead. Adjustable base plates can be added to the legs for 10 to 20 inches of leveling adjustment. Extension legs up to 36 inches long clamp on to compensate for more severe dips in the ground.

End frames are connected by bridging trestles or by diagonal crosspieces. A hoist standard, shown here lifting bricks in brick tongs, can lift up to 200 pounds of material to the top of the scaffold. A guardrail corrals the materials platform, and optional 2-by-6 toeboards prevent material from accidentally being kicked off.

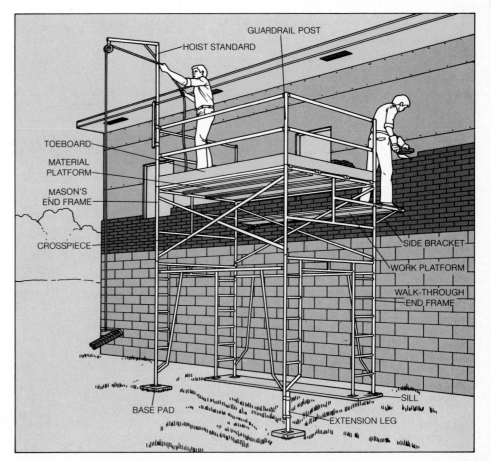

Point of departure. Suspended from a transit level, a brass plumb bob points to the precise center of a builder's reference stake. Centering the transit's plumb bob over a fixed point is the first step in setting up this precise and indispensable instrument, used to sight straight lines, measure horizontal and vertical angles, and position the strings that mark the boundaries for foundation walls and concrete footings.

In almost every part of the United States, anyone who plans to erect a sizable masonry structure will find that its design and construction are dictated by the local building code. These rules and regulations, which dictate safe building practices, are based on the known properties of building materials and their behavior under stress—typically, the stress exerted on a foundation slab by shifts in the soil beneath it. The local code spells out exactly what kinds of materials are to be used and how, and it specifies what characteristics the structural design must possess.

Most current building codes are based on one of three models published between 1927 and 1950, all of which were devised by companies and professionals associated with the building industry—insurance companies and manufacturers of building materials, as well as builders themselves. Initially, the codes were regional in scope, written for use in certain geographical zones by groups eager to maintain control over building regulations in their area. The Southern Building Code predominated in the southern states; the Uniform Building Code was devised for use on the West Coast; and the Basic Building Code was written for the Midwest and Northeast regions of the country. Despite their origins, each of these model codes is general enough to apply to all areas of the country.

Local codes, however, often are adaptations of the originals; they reflect the particular environmental demands of the area where they will be enforced. For example, the Basic Building Code requires that foundation footings and slabs rest below the frost line so that they will remain undisturbed by the heaving of topsoil in which ground water has frozen. But because the depth of the frost line varies widely from one area to another, the local codes call for a wide range of specifications—from 20 inches in most parts of Indiana to 6 feet underground in northern Maine.

From the footing up, the proposed masonry structure must satisfy code requirements in order to qualify for a building permit. In applying for the document, you will be asked to submit specifications and plans drawn to scale; the plans will be reviewed by a building-department engineer, who will determine whether your calculations are correct. For a sizable structure, these calculations can be complex, and it is advisable to enlist the help of a structural engineer in preparing them. Indeed, many building departments will refuse to review plans that have not been previously approved by a licensed engineer. And to proceed without a permit is foolhardy. Whether administered by the state, county or municipal government, a local building department has the authority to demolish any structure for which a permit has not been granted.

Marking Building Lines with Stakes and String

Every masonry project, from a simple garden wall to a new house, benefits from careful site preparation. Accurately laid-out building lines will not only save time and money during the course of the work, but may forestall possible structural or even legal complications. The dimensions of most footings and foundation walls, for example, are designed to take advantage of modular building materials, such as standard 8- or 16-inch concrete blocks; if the site is incorrectly laid out, the modules will have to be replaced with custom-cut materials. And if a building line is laid out slapdash, it may come closer to a property line than the law allows.

Before laying out any structure, you must locate your property line. In many cases, the surveying company that originally subdivided the acreage will have driven steel stakes at every corner of the lot. They may be hidden by vegetation or even buried under the soil, but a thorough search with a metal detector or a magnet will usually turn them up. If you cannot find the stakes, you must work from the property map—the plat—filed with the county zoning office when the land was sold. Often a copy of the plat accompanies the property deed.

The plat will show most of the permanent fixtures that were on the land when it was surveyed—utility poles, house walls, and the like. Using these for reference, you can locate your property lines. But these measurements may not be exact; if there is a chance that your building will violate setback laws or transgress a property line, have the land resurveyed and marked with corner stakes.

With the boundary lines established, prepare a sketch of the project to accompany your application for a building permit. Note all of the outside dimensions of your structure, including its height, and indicate the distances between the structure and the property line. With this information in hand, the building department will consider the plan, but it will send an inspector to the site to check your excavations before giving you approval to pour the concrete footings.

Before you excavate, you must transfer your plan from paper to the building site. To do so, you should be familiar with a few basic precepts of geometry and the methods by which surveyors employ the tools of their trade—stakes, strings, steel tapes, levels and transit levels.

For a small project on fairly level land, you can lay out your site by using the 3-4-5 method to square corners and a water level to check elevations. The 3-4-5 method is based on the fact that any triangle with sides 3, 4 and 5 units long—or multiples thereof—contains a right angle. The larger the multiples used, the more accurate the angle. A water level, available at building-supply stores, is simply a length of flexible transparent tubing filled with a mixture of antifreeze and water. You can make an adequate substitute by filling a transparent garden hose with water and clamping it at both ends. When a water level is stretched between stakes, the tubing fluid seeks its own level at both ends, and it can be used to set both stakes to the same height.

In the case of large structures, such as a house, or when working on land that is hilly, a surveyor's transit level is recommended, for both speed and accuracy. Although it can perform a variety of measuring tasks, you will use it primarily for sighting straight lines, measuring right angles and establishing identical elevations at various points on the site. You also will need a tripod that fits the base of the transit level, and a leveling rod—a long stick with graduated markings—to take elevation measurements. Transit levels and the accessories can be rented from surveying-equipment suppliers.

A major aim of your surveying is to set up corner markers, or batter boards—sets of stakes connected by horizontal boards. Set outside the building lines so that they will not interfere with construction, batter boards are referred to repeatedly throughout the foundation work. Strings are stretched between them for taking measurements, and the boards are often marked with dimensions and locations critical to the excavation and to building the foundation.

Batter boards should be set at a common level, if possible, to define a plane over the building site from which elevation measurements can be taken. Many builders set the boards at an arbitrary height, but you can simplify the task by setting them at the planned foundation height. When the project involves an addition to an existing house, set the batter boards level with the house foundation wall. The batter boards remain in place until the foundation is complete.

Laying Out a Site by the 3-4-5 Method

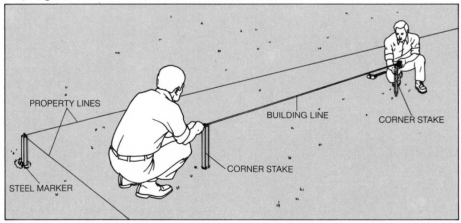

PROPERTY LINES

BUILDING LINE

CORNER STAKE

CORNER STAKE

STEEL MARKER

1 **Setting the first building line.** Drive a stake to mark the first corner of the planned building, starting with the corner nearest the property line; measure off the proposed length of one side of the building, and set a stake for the second corner. Stretch a string between nails driven into the top of two stakes, allowing an extra 5 feet of string to trail from each stake.

Measure between the stretched string and the property line to be sure the building line is far enough from the edge of the property.

To locate the property line, drive stakes just inside the steel corner markers placed by the surveyor, and run strings between nails driven into the top of the stakes.

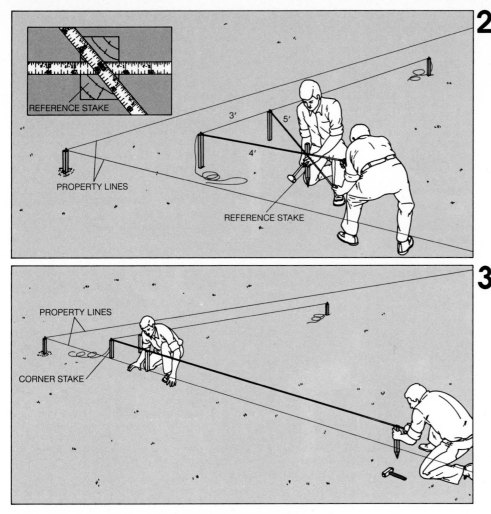

2 **Turning a corner.** To plot a right-angled corner for the second building line, drive a reference stake along the first building line 3 feet from the first corner stake. Hammer a nail into the top of the reference stake, exactly 3 feet from the nail in the corner stake. Have a helper hook a steel tape over each nail. Then the helper crosses the tapes and, holding one in each hand, pulls them out until the 4-foot mark on the corner-stake tape intersects the 5-foot mark on the other tape (*inset*). Drive a second reference stake at this point.

3 **Finishing the building lines.** Using the second reference stake and the corner stake as guides, string a second building line. Stretch a steel tape out from the corner stake to the planned length of the second line. Adjust the tape sideways until a helper, sighting over the reference stake, tells you it is centered. Drive a second corner stake here, and hammer a nail into its top. Tie the string between the two nails, again leaving an extra 5 feet trailing off from each stake. Check the measurements.

Using the technique shown in Step 2, make right angles at the remaining corners to complete the other two building lines. Check setbacks and remove property lines; remove all of the reference stakes, leaving the four corner stakes in place with strings attached.

Installing Batter Boards at the Corners

1 **Setting the stakes.** At each of the four corners of the building line, drive in a sturdy 2-by-4 stake, positioning it about 5 feet out in a diagonal line from the corner stake. Drive two more 2-by-4 stakes, each about 4 or 5 feet away from the first one and parallel to the two building lines. The length of the stakes may vary: They must be driven deep enough not to wobble, and they should reach several inches above the top of the planned foundation.

2 **Setting elevation lines.** On the outside surface of one 2-by-4 corner stake—the one at the highest corner if you are building on a slope—draw a line to mark the elevation of the planned foundation. Have a helper hold one end of a water level against this stake while you stretch the hose to each of the three remaining corner stakes in turn. At each, adjust the height of the hose until your helper signals that the water is level with the marked elevation line. Mark this level on each of the other three stakes.

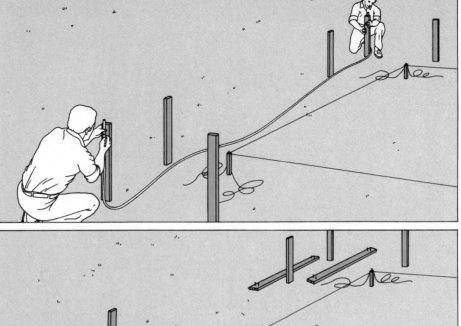

3 **Leveling the batter boards.** Cut two 1-by-6 boards, each long enough to run between the outer stakes and the corner. Start pairs of nails through the boards at points corresponding to the stakes. Hold the end of one board against the corner stake, lining up its top edge with the elevation line; drive one nail into the stake. Rest a carpenter's level on the edge of the board, and pivot the board on its single nail until it is truly horizontal. Secure the board to the outer stake with a single nail, then drive the remaining two nails. In the same way, attach a second batter board between the corner and the other outer stake. Then erect a pair of batter boards at each of the remaining three corners.

4 **Transferring construction lines.** Lift one of the building lines from its stake and pull it to the batter board. Have a helper line up a plumb bob with the nail on the stake and check the string for alignment while you secure it to the batter board with a nail. Repeat with all the remaining strings, which represent the outer foundation wall. Then remove the corner stakes that mark the building line.

Check the corners for squareness by measuring the distances from the string intersections corner to corner diagonally. If the distances are not identical, reposition the strings. At the same time, make sure that the length of the building lines remains correct. When the strings are in position, groove the top of the batter boards with a hand saw and pull the strings into the grooves. Or drive the nail into the batter board's top and loop the string around it. With the building lines in place, use them to measure and mark batter-board locations for string lines defining the inner face of the foundation wall and the two faces of the footings; nick each location with a saw to provide an anchor for the strings (inset). In loose or sandy soil, also include batter-board markings for the wider trench needed for the footing (page 40). Identify each construction line with a marking pencil.

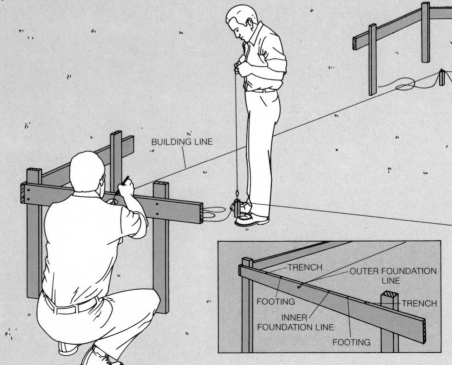

BUILDING LINE

TRENCH
OUTER FOUNDATION LINE
FOOTING
TRENCH
INNER FOUNDATION LINE
FOOTING

5 **Liming the lines.** Stretch string lines between the footing grooves on the batter boards—or, in sandy soils, between the trench grooves. Fill a plastic squeeze bottle with lime, and trim the bottle tip at an angle to produce a fairly wide line. Wearing gloves to protect your hands from the lime, dispense a line of lime on the ground directly beneath the string lines. For string lines within a foot or two of the ground, straddle the strings and work by eye. For strings too high to straddle, have a helper move ahead of you with a plumb bob while you dispense the lime. Remove the string lines for excavation.

Laying Out a Site with a Transit Level

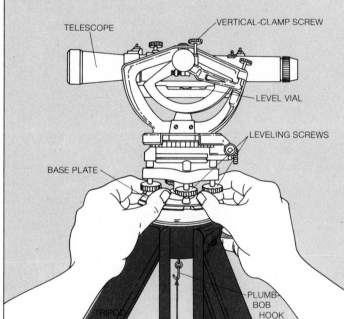

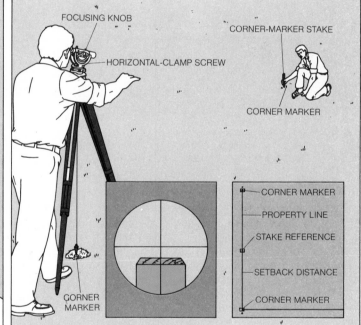

1 **Assembling and leveling the transit.** Twist the base plate into its socket. Spread the tripod legs and hang a plumb bob from the hook. Set the transit over a property-corner marker, adjusting it until the base plate is roughly level and the bob hangs near the center of the marker. Loosen the four leveling screws, slide the transit over the base plate until the plumb bob is centered over the marker, then tighten them.

Set the vertical scale to 0° and tighten the vertical-clamp screw to steady the telescope. Rotate the telescope to align with two opposite leveling screws; turn the screws in opposite directions, to center the bubble in the vial. Turn the telescope 90°, aligning it with two new leveling screws. Again turn the screws to center the bubble. Repeat twice more; the telescope should swing in a circle without moving the bubble.

2 **Setting a building-line reference point.** With the transit set over the first corner marker, have a helper hold a stake directly over the next corner marker along the property line. Focus the telescope until the stake aligns with the vertical cross hair *(inset, left);* ask the helper to mark the stake, then lock the horizontal-clamp screw. While you check for alignment, have your helper drive the stake into the ground in front of the marker. Put a nail into the stake top at the mark.

Without moving the transit, have your helper measure along the sighted line a distance equal to the planned setback of the building from the property line *(inset, right).* Set a reference stake, but have your helper move the stake to align with the vertical cross hair, then mark it where the cross hair hits it. Drive the stake; put a nail at the mark. Check your work through the telescope.

3 **Plotting the building corners.** Set up and level the transit over the setback reference stake established in Step 2, and sight from this point to the stake placed at the corner marker in Step 2; lock the horizontal-clamp screw. Depress the ring-mounted horizontal scale (inset) and turn it until one of the 0° or 90° marks lines up with the 0° mark on the fixed scale. Then unlock the horizontal-clamp screw and rotate the telescope 90°, until the fixed scale indicates that you have turned 90° on the horizontal scale. Using the same procedures as in Step 2, have a helper position a stake along the new sight line, at a distance equal to the planned setback of the building line from the first property line, established in Step 2. This stake marks the first corner of the building line.

Without moving the transit, have your helper set a second stake farther along the same sight line. The distance between the stakes should equal the planned length of that side of the building. Then move and level the transit over either of these two stakes, and sight to the opposite stake. Rotate the transit 90°, and have your helper set the third stake. Finally, move and level the transit over the third stake, and sight back to the second stake; then rotate the transit 90° and set the fourth stake. Check your work by measuring the dimensions of the layout.

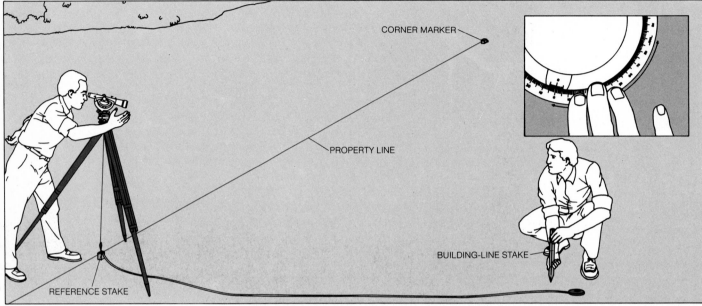

CORNER MARKER

PROPERTY LINE

BUILDING-LINE STAKE

REFERENCE STAKE

4 **Leveling the batter boards.** Drive stakes for batter boards at all four corners of the building line, as described in Step 1, page 29. Mark the foundation height—or an arbitrary elevation—on one stake, the one at the highest corner of the site if you are building on a slope. Set up and level the transit near the center of the site, and check it for level. Lock the telescope horizontally by setting the vertical scale on 0 and tightening the vertical-clamp screw. Have a helper hold a leveling rod against the marked stake, lining up the bottom of the rod with the elevation mark. Focus the telescope and read the number on the rod that coincides with the horizontal cross hair (inset). Record this number, which represents the difference in plane between the elevation mark and the locked telescope position.

Have a helper move the leveling rod to another corner stake, and swing the transit to focus on the rod in that position. Direct the helper to raise or lower the rod against the stake until the recorded number coincides with the horizontal cross hair. Mark the corner stake at the bottom of the leveling rod. Repeat this procedure at each of the remaining two stakes. Then nail level batter boards to the stakes, using the marks as guides, and add notches for construction lines, as described in Step 4, page 30.

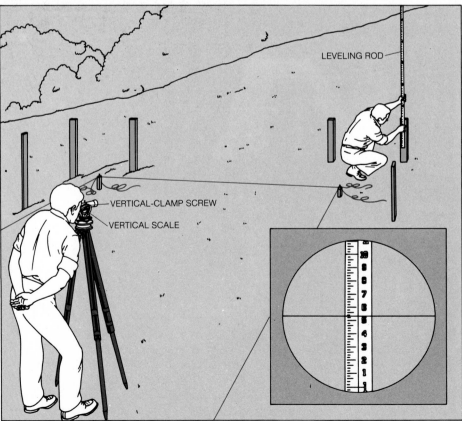

LEVELING ROD

VERTICAL-CLAMP SCREW

VERTICAL SCALE

A Stepped Footing for a Hillside

When a lot slopes steeply, you can save on excavation and concrete with a footing that descends in a series of stepped slabs resembling a giant double stairway. If you plan to erect a concrete-block wall on the footing, the steps' risers must be in multiples of 8 inches—the height of one course of concrete block—so that the blocks will rise level with each tier of steps. The exact length of the steps is not crucial, but for structural reasons it should be at least 2 feet.

To lay out a stepped footing, you need a leveling rod to locate and mark the 8-inch changes along your building lines. Using these marks, you can then lime the ground at every level where you want the excavator to dig to a different depth.

1 **Measuring grade changes.** Stretch strings along the outer building lines running down the slope, using the notched markings on the batter boards as guides. Beginning at the downhill end of one string and gradually working uphill, measure the distance between the string and the ground with a leveling rod. Wherever the level changes 8 inches, drive a stake.

To measure grade changes with a transit, set up the instrument inside the site, level it and lock the telescope vertically. Have a helper stand a leveling rod on the ground next to the lowest corner stake; read the scope, noting the number on the rod that meets the horizontal cross hair. Continue to read the scope as the helper walks uphill. Wherever the grade level rises 8 inches, have your helper drive a stake. Check your work.

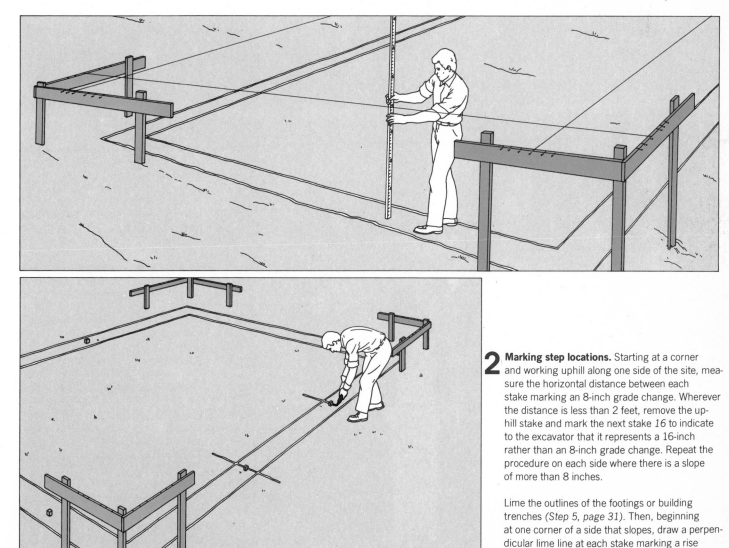

2 **Marking step locations.** Starting at a corner and working uphill along one of the site, measure the horizontal distance between each stake marking an 8-inch grade change. Wherever the distance is less than 2 feet, remove the uphill stake and mark the next stake *16* to indicate to the excavator that it represents a 16-inch rather than an 8-inch grade change. Repeat the procedure on each side where there is a slope of more than 8 inches.

Lime the outlines of the footings or building trenches (*Step 5, page 31*). Then, beginning at one corner of a side that slopes, draw a perpendicular lime line at each stake marking a rise in grade. Extend the grade lines 2 feet beyond each side of the trench or footing lines.

Rough-grading and Excavating a Building Site

Even a relatively small excavation for a concrete slab or footing often requires a substantial amount of digging. Although a hand-operated power trencher can quickly dig narrow, clean-sided footing trenches as deep as 5 feet, most jobs are much better done with larger earth-moving machines. The saving in time usually more than offsets the expense of renting the machine.

The standard machines for moving earth are bulldozers, front-end loaders and backhoes. A bulldozer is best suited for grading—leveling uneven terrain. Its broad, flat blade can be raised or lowered to cut and push earth. A tire- or track-mounted front-end loader can be used for grading, but its broad scoop is better for picking up spoil—excavated earth—and loading it onto a truck for removal.

A backhoe, the machine most used for all but the largest excavations, is a power shovel that can move 25 yards of earth an hour. It is a versatile piece of equipment that can sculpt an embankment to the proper slope, cut wide, deep trenches, and dig more precisely than either a front-end loader or a bulldozer. Tractors are often equipped with a front-end loader and backhoe attachments, so that one machine can grade, load and dig with equal effectiveness.

Before breaking ground with any of these machines, you must know what to expect below the surface. Check with your local utility agencies to determine the exact location of water and sewer lines; these agencies provide charts or on-site staking for their underground lines. If you plan an excavation deeper than the soft, workable layer of topsoil, have an engineer take a soil bore or a core sample; these tests will indicate if the topsoil masks a subsurface of stony soil or solid rock. Excavating in stone must be done by professionals, which will cost three to five times as much as digging in more workable soil.

Before excavation, unimproved lots often require preliminary grading to provide a relatively even working surface. The boundaries of the rough-graded area can be any that you choose; they need not be laid out as precisely as the perimeter of a foundation. The level of the grade should be established in reference to a known elevation (usually indicated on builder's plans). At various points around the area, you must indicate the amount of earth to be cut or filled, to guide the grading-equipment operator. You may also have to clear the ground before grading, removing brush and trees, then having the remaining stumps either pulled or blasted out by a professional.

Whether or not you rough-grade the area prior to excavating, you will need to set up batter boards as reference points for the actual digging (page 30). These will be keyed to the elevation of the planned foundation and will be marked with footing or foundation lines, which can then be transferred to the ground with lime (page 31). Make sure the boundaries of the planned excavation include space for shoring, if required (page 38), outside the building lines.

If you want to save topsoil scraped off during grading, select a spot for it to be piled, away from excavation and construction so that it will not have to be repeatedly moved. If you do not plan to use topsoil or spoil from the excavation, you will have to rent a truck or hire a contractor to haul it away; be sure to save some spoil for backfilling the excavation once the structure is finished.

Most earth-moving machines can be rented from an excavating contractor on an hourly or daily basis. The contractor will explain the functions and operation of the different machines and deliver them to the site, usually at additional cost. Be sure that you understand all maintenance requirements, such as levels for oil and hydraulic fluid, since lack of these fluids can ruin a machine.

Although some machines are quite simple to operate, large backhoes and bulldozers can buck and bounce and may easily knock the corner off a house if improperly or carelessly handled. If you have no experience operating heavy equipment, it is best to hire a professional operator. Not only is it safer, but speed and accuracy are likely to be greater. In fact, for some excavations, professional help is essential. If the hole is to be larger and deeper than 4 feet, or close to an existing building, hire a professional. The fee will be determined by the size of the cut, the rock content of the soil, the distance spoil must be hauled, and the time required for digging and shoring.

GROUND-LEVEL LINE

Protection for Tree Trunks

Wrapping and banding a trunk. Pad any trees that are to be saved with several layers of thick cloth or newspaper to a height of 4 feet. Surround the padding with a closely spaced paling of 1-by-4 boards, and fasten it at top and bottom with baling wire.

Paint a white band around the trunk at ground level, to indicate where the roots begin. Should the base of the trunk be temporarily buried, use the painted band to keep from digging too deep and damaging the roots.

Marking Grade Stakes for Changes in Elevation

1 Setting the grade stakes. Lay out the perimeter of the area to be graded with 2-by-4 stakes 3 feet long, placed at 30-foot intervals. Using a transit level, measure the depth of earth to be cut or filled at each stake for a level grade. Set up and level the transit outside the lowest part of the area (*inset*); then set the scope at 0° vertical. Have a helper hold a leveling rod against the ground at the reference-elevation point noted on the blueprint or building plan; focus the transit on the rod and record the reading. Then compute the difference between this reading and the rough-grade level indicated on the plan, keyed to the reference elevation. When you have computed this difference, make a note of it; it will be used as a reference reading.

Have your helper hold the leveling rod against the ground at one of the perimeter stakes, and pivot the transit to focus on it. Take a reading and note the difference between this reading and the reference reading, indicating with a plus or minus whether it is higher or lower. Transfer this figure to the grading plan. Perform similar computations for each perimeter stake.

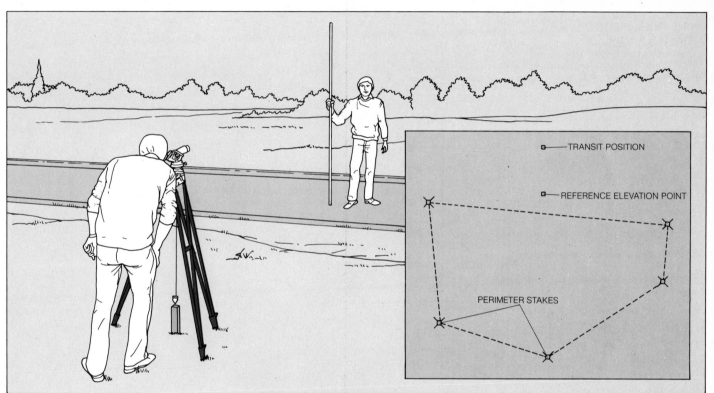

TRANSIT POSITION

REFERENCE ELEVATION POINT

PERIMETER STAKES

2 Marking the stakes. With a felt-tipped marker, draw a line at ground level on each perimeter stake, and above the line put a small arrow pointing downward; this will enable you to locate the line as the earth is moved. Label each stake with a *C*, if the earth is to be cut away at that point, or an *F*, if the excavator should fill there. Using the plus and minus figures noted on the grading plan, indicate the amount of earth to be cut or filled at each stake. Be sure to mark the stakes clearly enough for the excavator to read them from the machine.

GROUND-LEVEL LINE

Monitoring the Depth of an Excavation

1 | **Establishing the proper depth.** Set up and mark batter boards as described on pages 28-33, and use them to scribe chalk lines on the ground, defining the edge of the cut. With the backhoe positioned near one corner, the operator will make a cut along the perimeter of the excavation and then make successive overlapping cuts in a fan pattern toward the center *(inset)*. Check the depth of the excavation from time to time by having a helper stretch strings between the tops of the batter boards; measure from the strings to the excavation floor, using a folding rule or a long, marked pole. When the excavation is within 1 inch of the desired depth, the backhoe should be moved to a new location; remove and replace the strings as needed in order to keep them out of the way of the backhoe.

Check for depth periodically as the backhoe continues to dig around the edge of the excavation. Although the excavation can extend a few inches beyond the chalk lines without consequence, it must not exceed the proper depth.

2 | **Checking depths across the center.** Stretch a string between the batter boards at two adjacent corners, and anchor it securely. Attach a second string to a batter board on the opposite side of the excavation, and swing it across the excavation to meet the fixed string. Have a helper hold this reference string against the fixed string while you use a folding rule or a marked pole to measure the depth of the excavation at various points along the reference string. Then have your helper swing the reference string to another location along the fixed string, and again take depth readings. Continue in this way, mapping the depth over the center of the excavation floor at 10-foot intervals. Sprinkle chalk to mark any high points for the backhoe to remove.

REFERENCE STRING

FIXED STRING

3 Smoothing the walls and floor. Working with a blunt-ended shovel, shave off the remaining 1 inch of soil from the excavation floor, bringing the floor to its proper depth and at the same time leveling its surface. To make sure the floor is level, lay a long straight 2-by-4 across it, with a mason's level on top.

If the depth of the excavation exceeds the amount specified, do not attempt to raise it with backfill. Instead, plan to increase the depth of the concrete footing to compensate for the error.

A Power Tool That Cuts Trenches Quickly

Operating a power trencher. Mark the trench outlines with lime *(page 31)*, creating a pathway for the trencher, and clear the pathway of stones and other obstacles. Position the trencher on the pathway, start the motor and engage the clutch that controls the movement of the chain-linked scoops around the slanted digging boom. With the scoops in motion, turn the depth-adjustment wheel counterclockwise to set the boom for the desired depth of cut. Lock the depth wheel and, if the engine speed is adjustable, increase the speed until the chain revolves smoothly, without dragging, and the scoops carry a full load of dirt without stalling. Change the engine speed as necessary to maintain this balance.

Guide the trencher backward along the lime-marked pathway until the front wheels have reached the corner. Then disengage the chain clutch, raise the boom and reposition the trencher on the adjacent section of the pathway. Repeat this process until you have circumnavigated the trench. Clean out the corners of the trench with a shovel. If you are making a cut wider than the cutting width of your trencher, you will have to make a separate cut 4 inches to one side of the original trench, then clean out the remaining strip of earth with a shovel.

Caution: Never reach under or near the digging boom while the motor is on. Switch off the motor before checking the depth of the cut.

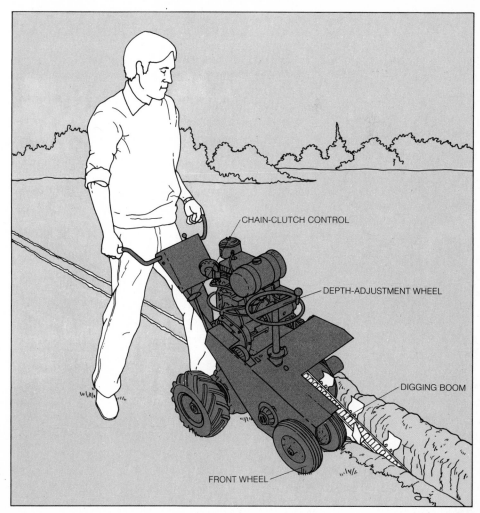

CHAIN-CLUTCH CONTROL

DEPTH-ADJUSTMENT WHEEL

DIGGING BOOM

FRONT WHEEL

Shoring the Excavation Walls for Safety

Anyone who has peered through peepholes provided for sidewalk superintendents at urban construction sites has undoubtedly noticed the fortress-like shoring along the sides of the pit. This heavy framework of steel pilings and massive wood beams and braces prevents the walls of the excavation from caving in under the weight of surrounding buildings. Such protective measures are an extreme, but cave-ins always pose a threat when you work below ground, and virtually any excavation more than 4 feet deep must employ some form of bank stabilization—sloping the bank, shoring, or a combination of the two. Only stone, or stone-hard soils that show no cracks, may be left vertically cut.

The simplest way to stabilize a bank is to slope it. The angle of slope is determined by the stability of the soil. Firm cemented, hardpan layers and compacted, stony soil can be left unsupported if sloped to an angle of at least 80°. Medium soils, such as moist clays and hardened sands, should be cut to a 60° angle; soft topsoil, humus, sand and wet clay must be angled to at least 45°. A structural engineer can determine your soil type and the required slope angle.

In some cases, sloping may be impractical because of the depth of the excavation or the proximity of other structures or trees. The type of shoring required under these circumstances is determined by a combination of factors: soil type, depth of cut, and possible threat to nearby structures. Skip shoring, the simplest method, is used only in relatively hard soil that is cut no deeper than 10 feet and shows no evidence of crumbling or collapsing. It is made by bracing single vertical planks against the bank at regular intervals. In hard soil, set the planks at 8-foot intervals; in medium-hard soils, at 3-foot intervals.

Close shoring, used in medium to soft soils, has vertical planks placed close together and braced from behind with horizontal members called wales, vertical members called strongbacks and diagonal bracing. A third method is tight shoring, similar to close shoring except that the vertical planks are firmly butted and seated in a trench to anchor them at the base of the wall. Close or tight shoring is also needed in any excavation near a building or thoroughfare, but such a job requires professional expertise.

Because shoring must restrain great forces, the sheathing planks must be at least 2 inches thick. Heavy beams, no smaller than 4-by-6, are required for the horizontal wales and vertical strongbacks, and each diagonal brace must be a 6-by-6 beam or doubled 2-by-10 planks, one on each side of the strongback. Unless you will be able to put this heavy, expensive timber to use later, it is best to rent a shoring system. Rental systems are available from some excavation firms or from rental agencies that supply professional contractors. Assemble the shoring with 16-penny (3½-inch) double-headed nails, large enough to hold securely and yet easy to remove when the construction is complete.

As you erect the shoring, keep a close eye on the walls of the excavation. Cave-ins seldom occur immediately after excavation, but time and changes of weather can cause an unshored bank to crumble. Inspect the banks carefully after rains for signs of fissures or slumping—wet soil, dangerously heavy and slippery, is a major cause of cave-ins. Dryness can also be a problem, especially in sandy soils. Previously disturbed soil, even when solidly tamped, does not bind well and is susceptible to the vibrations of heavy earth-moving equipment, as are the corners formed by intersecting trenches.

Exercise great care when you remove shoring, since the soil it restrains may have dried out or crumbled. Contractors often avoid the risk of pulling shoring by simply burying the lumber. A more economical method is to remove the bracing as you backfill the excavation when building is complete. As the backfill approaches the level of a shoring member, pull it out of the fill from above with the backhoe. Leave in place any pieces that cannot be pulled out.

Skip-Shoring for Firm Soil

Setting up a braced plank. Brace each 2-by-10 plank against the bank with 4-by-6 horizontal and diagonal beams, and secure each beam with a 2-by-4 stake. Butt the horizontal brace against the bottom of the plank. Nail a 2-by-4 cleat about 6 inches below the top of the plank, and wedge the diagonal brace, beveled at one end to 45°, under the cleat. Nail the diagonal brace to the plank. Cut the other end of this brace square, making it even with the end of the horizontal brace. Drive the stake 2 feet into the ground, behind the braces, to hold the plank against the bank. Nail through the stake into the horizontal and diagonal braces to secure them.

Tight Shoring for Soft Soil

1 Setting the supporting frame. Dig a narrow trench 1 foot deep around the perimeter of the excavation. Assemble one section of supporting frame by laying a pair of parallel 4-by-6 wales on the ground, narrow faces up; space the wales so that they will be 2 feet above the excavation floor and 1 foot below ground level when the shoring is erected. Nail a 2-by-10 control plank across each end of the wales to hold them in place, and stand this frame upright against the bank, with the bottoms of the control planks in the trench. Toenail vertical 4-by-6 strongbacks to the wales at 8-foot intervals, narrow faces out.

Assemble enough frames to enclose the excavation. Wherever sections of wale join, strengthen the joint with a strongback. Brace the strongbacks temporarily to hold the control planks securely against the wall, using diagonal 2-by-4 braces held in place by short 2-by-4 stakes.

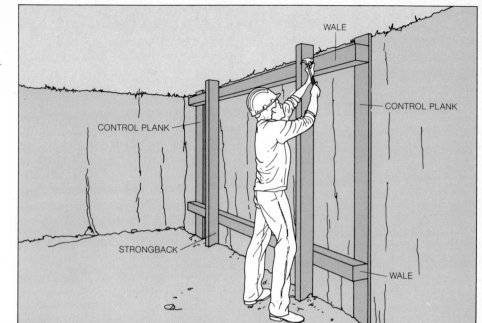

2 Placing the sheathing. Slide a 2-by-12 sheathing plank between the wales and the bank, butting it tightly against a control plank. Tap the sheathing plank with a sledge to seat it in the bottom of the trench. Then continue placing sheathing planks, side by side, around the excavation. Use planks of varying lengths to support the bank where its height varies and narrow planks as necessary to fit the gap between the line of sheathing and the control plank.

3 Completing the shoring. Working at one strongback at a time, remove the temporary 2-by-4 brace and replace each one with a pair of diagonal 2-by-10 braces, nailed at one end to the sides of the strongback and at the other to a 4-by-4 stake. Position each brace at a 45° angle to the strongback, with its end butting against the corner of the top wale; nail it in place. Drive the 4-by-4 stake about 2 feet into the ground between the pair of braces, at a right angle to them; nail the braces to the stake. Wedge two short 2-by-4 stakes immediately behind the 4-by-4 stake to force the shoring against the bank (*inset*). Then drive a 2-by-4 stake against the bottom of strongback, and fill in the trench to bury the bottom of the sheathing.

Constructing a Solid Footing for Masonry

A house foundation is only as strong as the footing it stands on. This concrete pad carries the weight of the foundation down to the solid, unexcavated soil below the frost line. In addition, a footing performs two other crucial jobs: Its level top provides a firm, flat surface on which to build, and its width, generally twice that of the foundation, distributes the load of the foundation over a greater area of bearing soil.

The dimensions of the footing are determined by the local building code. The blueprint, prepared by an engineer, will specify the exact width of the footing as well as its thickness. For a residential building, the footing is typically 8 inches thick, although footings for piers may be as deep as 3 feet to get near grade level. In areas where the soil is compact and contains a lot of clay, the trench or hole dug for the footing will also serve as a form for the concrete. All you need to add are grade pegs to indicate the footing height; made of steel reinforcing bar, or rebar, grade pegs are set into the earthen form so that their tops are level with the planned top of the footing.

Where soil is sandy or unstable, you will need to build wooden footing forms to shape the concrete, but you can eliminate the grade pegs, since the top of the forms will indicate the footing height. To make the footing forms, you will need 1-inch-thick lumber as wide as the footing is thick; for an 8-inch footing, for example, you will need 1-by-8 boards. Because a 1-by-8 is only 7½ inches wide, the forms must be raised ½ inch off the ground, but such small gaps can just be packed with earth before the concrete is poured.

Curved footings, such as those that underpin the serpentine wall on page 108, are generally shaped from ¼-inch hardboard instead of 1-inch lumber. For very tight curves, you may have to use ⅛-inch hardboard, which is easier to bend. For added strength, nail a second strip of ⅛-inch hardboard to the back of the first.

After the grade pegs or forms are in place, the footing is reinforced with horizontal lengths of rebar. Although local codes differ on the size and spacing of the rebar, most call for ½-inch rebar for residential projects and specify that it be laid in two parallel rows, like railroad tracks, along the length of the trench. To go around corners, the rebar must be bent. This is easily done by means of a length of metal pipe used as a bending sleeve. When lengths of rebar need to be joined, overlap them about 15 inches, and lash them together at three points with 18- or 20-gauge steel tie wire.

For some footings, such as those that step up a hillside (page 33), vertical as well as horizontal rebar will be needed, sized and spaced as required by the building code. Stepped footings also need baffles—additional form boards to shape the concrete along the front edge of each step. The baffles are cut from strips of ¾-inch plywood, as wide as the steps are high and about 3 inches longer than the width of the steps, so that the ends of the baffles can be wedged into the earth. The height of each step and of its baffle can be 8, 16 or 24 inches; the top of each baffle can serve as a grade level for the poured concrete, but grade pegs will make the job easier.

To place the baffles, use the trench floor for the bottom step as a reference point. The bottom edge of the first baffle should be the same distance above the trench floor as the planned thickness of the footing. Because the slabs of the footing will overlap by about 1 foot, this first baffle will actually have to sit about 1 foot forward of the vertical rise of the dirt excavation.

With the forms and rebar in place, you must arrange to have the work inspected by the local building department. Meanwhile, you can estimate how much concrete you will need. Multiply the length, width and thickness of the footing to get its volume in cubic feet; then convert this into cubic yards—the form in which concrete is sold—by dividing it by 27.

The most convenient way to buy large amounts of concrete is from a transit-mix company, which will mix the concrete to your specifications and deliver it, ready to pour, to the site. Most footings call for air-entrained concrete, a more expensive mixture that includes thousands of tiny air bubbles, which allow the concrete to expand and contract without cracking. Usually a mixture that contains 4 per cent air is sufficient, but in areas with particularly severe climates, 6 per cent air entrainment may be recommended.

Another variable is the consistency—called slump—of the concrete. Ask the supplier for a "medium-grade concrete for footings," and the firm will know the proper mix for your region. For stepped footings, however, ask for a slightly stiffer mixture, with a little less water, so that the concrete will set up faster and be better able to support the weight of the concrete above it.

Just before the transit-mix truck arrives, spray the inside of the forms with water; this will prevent them from drawing water from the concrete. Because of their small surface area, they need not be coated with form oil.

If possible, have the truck back right up to the footing trench to pour the concrete. If the truck must park in the street and disgorge its contents into wheelbarrows, lay down a ramp of 2-inch-thick boards between the truck and the trench. Also, enlist the aid of several helpers to serve as a wheelbarrow brigade; some transit-mix companies levy a surcharge for long delays.

As the footing is poured, it must be smoothed with a float. A keyed footing, which has a center groove that interlocks with a poured-concrete wall (page 45), must be smoothed and then grooved. The concrete should be loosely covered with plastic sheeting to keep it moist. After the concrete has set, in approximately 24 hours, the sheeting and form boards can be removed and the foundation work can begin.

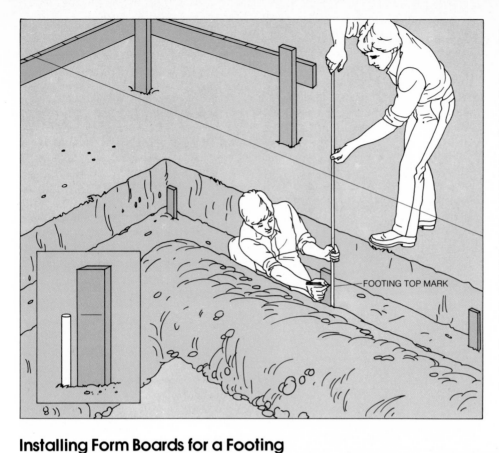
FOOTING TOP MARK

A Packed-Earth Form for Poured Concrete

Setting rebar grade pegs. Excavate the footing trench to the required depth. Place one stake at each corner; then, 3 inches in from either side of the trench, drive stakes at 3-foot intervals, alternating sides to make a zigzag pattern. Mark the grade level for the footing on each stake. To determine the grade-level markings, calculate the distance between the top of the footing and the top of the foundation; both these heights will be on the blueprint or building plan. Then restring one line between the batter boards *(pages 29-31)*, so that it comes above the inner row of stakes. Measure down from this string, which marks the foundation top, to locate the footing top. Have a helper hold a leveling rod or a folding ruler against the string while you transfer the footing measurement to one stake. Then transfer this grade mark to the other stakes, using a water level.

Drive a length of rebar into the ground beside the stake, until the top of the rebar is level with the grade mark *(inset)*. Remove the stakes and tamp the earth firmly around the rebar.

Installing Form Boards for a Footing

1 Installing the outside form boards. Excavate the footing trench to the required depth, and set two 2-by-4 support stakes at one corner. To position the stakes, restring the lines marking the outside edge of the footing on the batter boards. Drop a plumb bob where the strings intersect. Measure back from that point a distance equal to the thickness of the form boards, and drive in the two stakes at a right angle to each other *(above, left)*.

Set support stakes at 3-foot intervals down the length of the trench and at each corner, using the string line and the plumb bob to find their positions. Then mark the footing level on the stakes as at top. Attach form boards to the insides of the stakes, level with the footing marks. Secure them with double-headed nails, backing the boards with a heavy hand sledge to steady them for nailing *(above, right)*. Set an extra support stake at any joint between form boards.

2 **Building the inside forms.** Using the outside form boards for reference, set a pair of 2-by-4 support stakes at each corner and individual stakes at 3-foot intervals down the length of the trench. To position the stakes, measure in from the outside form boards a distance equal to the width of the footing plus the thickness of the form boards. To mark the footing level on the stakes, hold a carpenter's level between each stake and the top of the outside form. Nail form boards to the inside stakes as in Step 1.

Brace all the support stakes with diagonal 1-by-4s anchored to outrigger stakes *(inset)*. Before pouring the concrete, pack earth halfway up the outside of the forms to provide extra strength.

Building Curved Forms

Laying out stakes in a curve. Draw two parallel lime lines down the middle of the trench, reproducing the excavation curves; space the lines as far apart as the width of the footing. Drive support stakes 1 foot apart and ½ inch outside the lines, narrow edges facing in. Mark the level for the footing top on one stake, as on page 41. Transfer this marking to the other stakes.

Cut hardboard the height of the footing. For gentle curves, use ¼-inch hardboard; for tighter curves, two thicknesses of ⅛-inch hardboard. Nail it to the stakes, its top even with the footing-level marks *(page 41, Step 1)*. Push earth about halfway up the form to brace it.

LIME LINES

Adding Reinforcement

Providing horizontal support. Place lengths of rebar parallel to each other along the trench, spacing them the required distance apart. Set pieces of brick or small rocks under the rebar about every 8 feet to lift the rebar approximately 3 inches above the trench floor. In an earth-formed footing, lash the rebar to the grade pegs with steel tie wire. In a wood-formed footing, use bolt cutters to cut short pieces of rebar for cross ties and lash them to the rebar *(inset)*; space the cross ties about 4 feet apart. Where lengths of rebar join, overlap their ends about 15 inches for ½-inch rebar, more for larger rebar. Lash them together with tie wire.

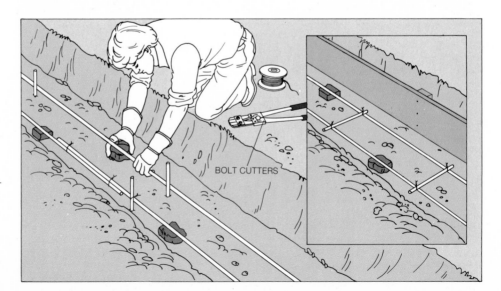

BOLT CUTTERS

Reinforcing independent footings. To reinforce a footing for a foundation pier or post, cut six lengths of rebar 6 inches shorter than the dimensions of the excavation. Lash them together in a crisscross pattern with tie wire; center the resulting grid in the excavation, setting it about 3 inches above the earth on pieces of brick or rock. Install grade pegs to mark the thickness of the footing, as on page 41.

Shaping Rebar for Special Fittings

Bending rebar with a pipe sleeve. Place a length of rebar on the ground and slip a length of steel pipe over one end. Press your foot against the rebar, just beyond the pipe sleeve, and slowly pull up the pipe sleeve toward you.

Setting in vertical rebar. For stepped footings (*above, left*), measure the rise and run of the excavated steps and bend rebar to match their contours. When necessary, join sections of rebar on the horizontal runs. Prop the horizontal sections of rebar with rocks or bricks so that they are 3 inches off the excavation floor, and set the vertical sections 3 inches away from the vertical faces of the steps. Lash the rebar to the grade pegs to fix it in position.

Where vertical rebar must protrude from a footing to anchor a retaining wall (*pages 94–97*), bend the rebar at right angles. Lash one leg to the horizontal rebar, the vertical leg to the grade peg to hold it up while the concrete is poured.

Placing the Baffles for a Stepped Footing

1 Marking baffle locations. Measure 1 foot out from the front of each excavated step, and mark a lime line 10 to 12 inches long at a right angle to the trench. Drive two parallel support stakes diagonally into the side of the trench at every mark. Sink the stakes at least 1 foot into the earth, leaving about 8 inches protruding.

Measure the trench width at the stakes. Cut ½-inch plywood baffles 3 inches longer than the width of the trench and as wide as the step will be high—but in 8-inch multiples. For the top step in the trench, double that height so that the baffle top will also serve as a grade peg.

2 Leveling the baffles. Set grade pegs and rebar in the trench (*page 41, top, and page 43, bottom*), then wedge the baffles into the trench on the uphill side of the support stakes. Using a sledge hammer, force each baffle down until its bottom edge is the same number of inches above the trench floor as the planned thickness of the footing—the bottom edge should be exactly aligned with the top of the grade pegs.

Hold a carpenter's level against the face of each baffle to check it for plumb and against the top edge to check it for level. Then nail the baffles to their support stakes.

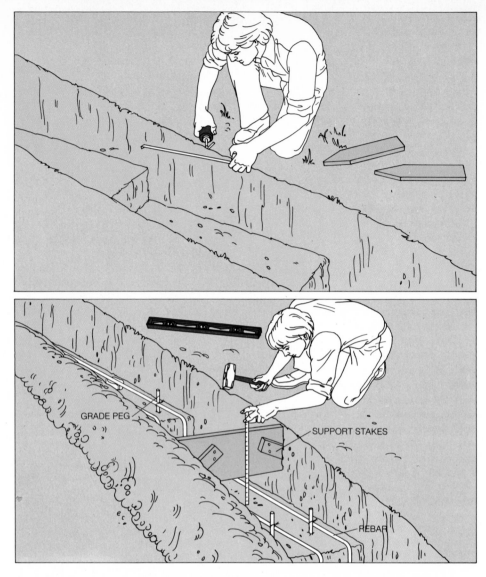

GRADE PEG

SUPPORT STAKES

REBAR

Pouring Concrete into the Prepared Forms

Pouring a level footing. As you dump the concrete into the trench, have your helper spread it evenly between the trench walls or the wooden forms, using a shovel, a hoe or a rake. Continue pouring until the concrete just reaches the tops of the grade pegs or forms. Lightly tamp the concrete with a 2-by-4 to settle it, or tap the outside of the forms with a rubber mallet.

Pouring a stepped footing. Fill the lowest level of the trench to the top of the grade pegs *(opposite, bottom)*, using a hoe or a shovel to push concrete under the first baffle. Tamp the concrete and let it set for 15 to 30 minutes. Move uphill 2 feet behind the first baffle and pour the next step. Push the concrete under the second baffle, and pull it against the first baffle until it is level with the baffle top and with the grade pegs. Again, tamp the concrete and let it set for 15 to 30 minutes. Continue pouring and leveling the concrete into each step up the slope until the entire footing is poured.

WOOD FLOAT

GRADE PEGS

Finishing the Footing

Smoothing the surface. Smooth the concrete with a wood float until the tops of the grade pegs just show. If you used forms, first screed the concrete level with the top of the form, using a 2-by-4 long enough to span the form's top edges. Then smooth the concrete with a wood float.

If the footing is to be keyed, let the concrete set only 15 to 30 minutes before shaping the key *(below)*. Otherwise, let the footing set 24 hours before beginning to erect the foundation on top of it. During that 24 hours, cover the footing loosely with plastic sheeting to keep it moist, or mist it every four hours with water.

Forming a key. After the concrete has set up slightly, drag a 2-by-4, wide side down, along the center of the footing to carve out a groove about 2 inches deep. Let the footing set for 24 hours, as above. Then begin preparations for pouring the concrete wall *(pages 52-61)*.

Shaping a Slab to Combine Footing and Floor

Most small single-story buildings, such as garages and garden sheds, can be built on a shaped concrete slab that combines footing with flooring. Called a turned-down slab—for its trenched edge—this dual-purpose construction can incorporate floor drains and other utility connections, as well as insulation. You can also build in reinforcements, called grade beams, which allow you to carry the slab over marshy ground, unstable soil or shallow tree roots.

Because the slab is poured in a single unit, careful planning and site preparation must precede the pour to ensure success. Even before you design the slab, check to be sure that local soil conditions and building codes permit a turned-down slab. Some codes require the perimeter footing to be dug to the frost line, but many soils are not stable enough to maintain the shape of a footing trench deeper than 2 feet. If the soil is very sandy, the trench may not hold its shape to a depth of 16 inches—the minimum required for strength—unless you build forms (pages 41-42).

Site preparation for a turned-down slab is the same as for a standard slab (pages 34-37). For a 4-inch slab, common in most areas, the excavation should be about 8 inches deep and 2 feet wider, on each side, than the planned slab. Later, a footing trench will be dug near the edge of the excavation.

As with most concrete work, the wood forms, gravel base and steel reinforcement should be in place before the concrete arrives; so should the insulation and any utilities included in the plan. If you are planning a wood-frame structure, you must also position anchor bolts for attaching a sill plate (page 47, Step 3).

The forms that define the edge of the slab are made as for footings (pages 41-42). For the underpinnings of the slab, you will need enough ¾-inch gravel to cover the shallow area to a depth of 3 to 4 inches. In wet areas you will also need enough 6-mil polyethylene sheeting to lay between the subgrade and the gravel. The sheeting acts as a moisture barrier between the ground and the concrete. For insulation, you will need polystyrene foam panels to line the inner face of the trench and to rim the adjacent slab.

If you plan to install a drain, you will need a section of drainpipe of the diameter specified by your local code, long enough to reach from the drain opening to the nearest main drain, plus an elbow fitting to carry the drain to the planned floor level and a drain unit. The unit consists of a vented drain cover attached to a collar made of outdoor plastic pipe.

For reinforcement, you will need ½-inch rebar and tie wire for the footings and grade beams, and 10-gauge woven wire mesh in a 6-inch grid for the slab. This mesh comes in 5-foot-wide rolls. A building-supplies dealer will help you estimate how much of all these materials you need. To estimate the amount of gravel and concrete you will require for both the footing and slab, use the formula on page 40.

Order a concrete mixture recommended by your concrete dealer, and have it delivered in a transit-mix truck. On the day of delivery, have three helpers on hand. Two workers will be needed to pour and shovel the concrete into the form while a third pushes it into the footing trench and a fourth screeds, or levels, the concrete. For a simple screed, nail two 2-by-4 handles to a 10-foot 2-by-4.

Screeding a slab with a drain requires the special slope-forming techniques shown in Step 5, page 48. Finish the slab with a magnesium-bladed bull float, a magnesium hand float and a rectangular steel trowel, all of which are available from tool-rental agencies.

A Turned-down Slab with a Floor Drain

1 **Preparing the site.** Excavate the slab area to a depth of 8 inches and drive a stake to mark the location of the drain opening. Dig a 24-inch trench from this point to the nearest main drain, then remove the marking stake. Assemble drainpipe in the trench, with a vertical extension long enough to bring the drain opening almost as high as the top of the forms.

Erect 2-by-8 forms (page 41), aligning their inner faces with the building lines and their top edges with the planned height of the slab. Brace the forms as for a standard footing (page 42), at intervals no greater than 3 feet.

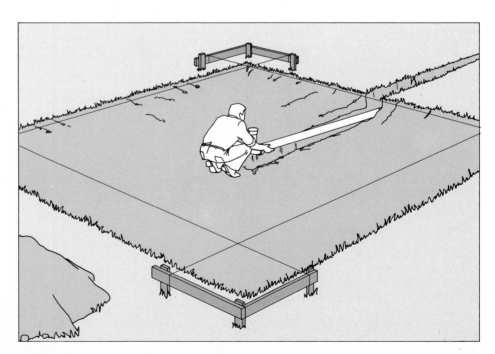

2 **Adjusting the drainpipe height.** Between two opposite form boards, stretch a string that passes over the drainpipe opening. Secure the string with nails at the top of each form. Measure the distance between the opening and the string—it should be great enough to allow for a downward pitch of ¼ inch per foot from the opening to the edge of the slab. Dig out or fill in the trench as needed to adjust the height of the drainpipe. Then fill in the trench to the level of the excavation, and tamp it firmly.

Brace the rim of the drain with two ½-inch rebar spikes, driven into the ground on opposite sides of the drain, just deep enough for the rim to rest on them. Tape plastic over the opening to protect it from the concrete during pouring.

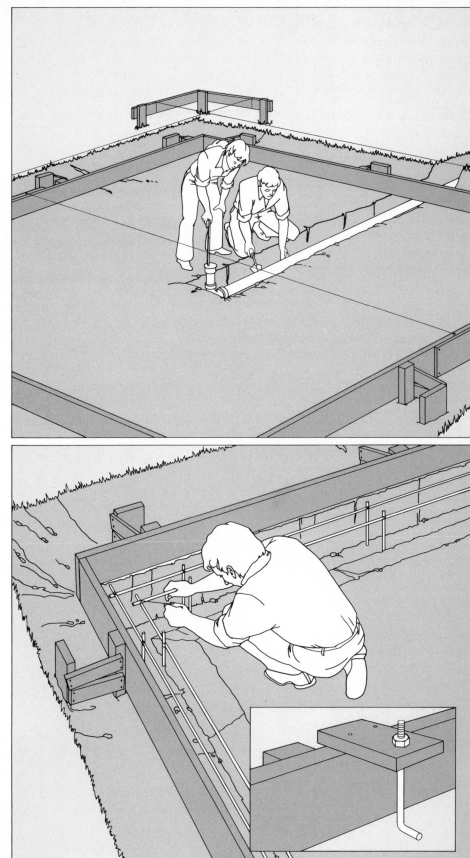

3 **Digging and reinforcing the trench.** Using the inner face of the form boards as a guide, dig a trench to the required depth around the perimeter of the slab area. The inner face of the trench should be angled so that the trench will measure 12 inches wide at the top and 7 inches at the bottom. Install a framework of ½-inch rebar in the trench, as on page 42. Place pairs of vertical rebar spikes, 6 inches apart, at 4-foot intervals; drive the spikes into the ground until they are 1 inch above the top of the trench. Wire horizontal sections of rebar to the spikes, 1 inch from the top; wire the horizontal sections of rebar together at the corners.

Cut 6-inch-long jigs for anchor bolts from 1-by-2 lumber; drill a ⅝-inch hole near one end of each jig. Fasten a ½-inch anchor bolt into each jig, but allow the bolt to protrude 2 inches above the surface of the jig. Nail the jigs to the top of the form at 4-foot intervals, positioning them so that the distance from the bolt to the inner face of the form is half the width of the planned sill plate (inset).

Cover the slab area, but not the trench, with a 3-inch layer of gravel. Screed the gravel.

4 **Insulating the slab.** Lay 1-inch-thick polystyrene foam panels along the inner face of the trench, cutting them so that their tops lie level with the gravel surface. Anchor the panels at the bottom of the trench, if necessary, with dirt. Lay additional panels along the edge of the slab area, extending inward about 2 feet.

Spread wire reinforcing mesh over the entire slab area and trench, ending about 2 inches in from the form boards. Position the mesh so that it fits over the drain. Wire the mesh to the rebar spikes (inset). As you spread the mesh, lay bricks under it at 3-foot intervals so that the mesh is suspended 2½ inches above the gravel.

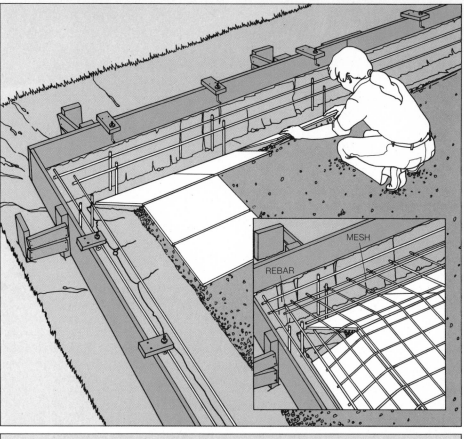

MESH

REBAR

5 **Filling the forms with concrete.** Pour and spread concrete inside the forms (pages 44-45), using shovels and rakes to push the concrete into place. Begin by filling around the drain, then work back, filling the remaining slab area and trench in wedge-shaped sections. As soon as one section is filled, level the concrete with a screed. To slope the concrete surface down to the drain, rest one end of the screed on the drain and the other atop the form boards. Grasp the screed handle and, as you walk backward, pull the screed toward you in an arc to smooth the surface and establish its downward slope. Remove the jigs holding the anchor bolts in place.

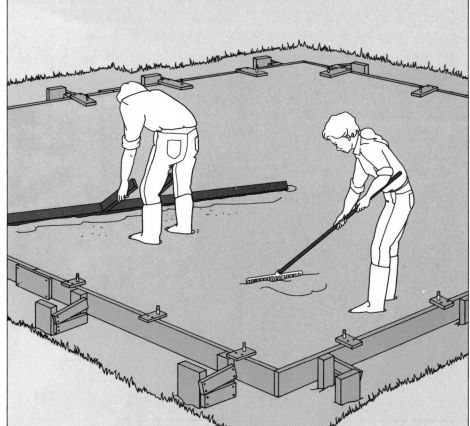

6 **Compacting the surface.** Compress and smooth the concrete with a bull float, beginning at the perimeter of the slab and working in toward the center. Stand outside and, with the length of the blade always pointing toward the drain, push the float in an arc as far as you can reach. As you push, tilt the front edge of the blade upward, then draw it back around the arc. On the backward pass, keep the blade flat against the concrete surface. Float adjacent areas of the slab in similar arcs, working in wedge-shaped sections and gradually moving from the edge of the slab to the center. Continue until you have floated the entire slab.

Stretch a string across the slab so that it passes over the drain. Allow water on the surface of the slab to evaporate before you continue.

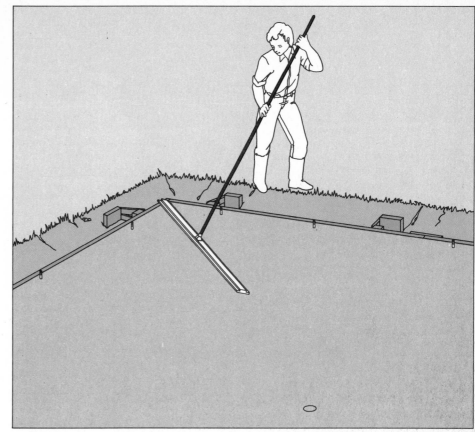

7 **Finishing the slab.** Use a trowel and a hand float to smooth the concrete surface into a gradual slope, checking the slope every few feet by measuring its distance from the string; it should rise about ¼ inch every foot. Begin at the drain and work out to the edge of the slab, working over one quadrant at a time. Sweep the slope in overlapping arcs, first with the float, then with the trowel. Fill in any depressions with wet concrete. To provide support as you work, kneel on a pair of knee boards—rectangles of ⅜-inch plywood with 2-by-2 handles at each end.

When the entire slab is smooth, wet it with a fine spray of water and cover it with overlapping sheets of 6-mil polyethylene to hold in moisture. Let the concrete cure for three days before removing the plastic and the forms.

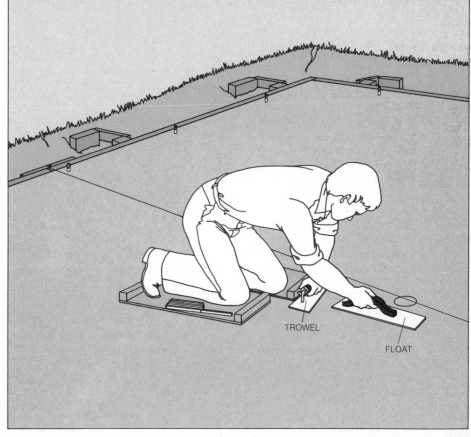

TROWEL

FLOAT

Underpinning with Poured-Concrete Grade Beams

A slab for shifting soil. To reinforce a turned-down slab built on marshy ground or on poorly compacted backfill, set grade beams within the slab area. Dig trenches across the slab area at 4-foot intervals, making them 12 inches wide and 8 inches deeper than the slab excavation and parallel to two sides of the footing trench. Lay rebar in the grade-beam trenches as on page 42, bracing the rebar with bricks placed in the bottom of the trench; add a second set of vertical spikes in the perimeter trench at its intersection with the grade beam, and wire the rebar to the spikes in the footing trench. Then add a second layer of bricks and rebar, tying the rebar to the vertical spikes in the footing trench. After the gravel, insulation and wire mesh are in place, tie the grade-beam rebar to the mesh at 2-foot intervals. Pour and finish the slab as in Steps 6-7, pages 48-49. If the slab has no drain, screed it as you would a footing (*page 40*), then float and trowel it as in Step 7, page 49.

A slab to bridge tree roots. When a turned-down slab passes over shallow tree roots that you do not wish to cut, substitute a grade beam for the section of footing trench that crosses the root system. Dig a footing trench to the required depth on either side of the root system, installing rebar as on page 42. Then span the roots with a grade-beam trench (*above*). Cover the slab with gravel, insulation and wire mesh (*page 47*), then tie the rebar in both the grade-beam trench and the footing trench to the wire mesh.

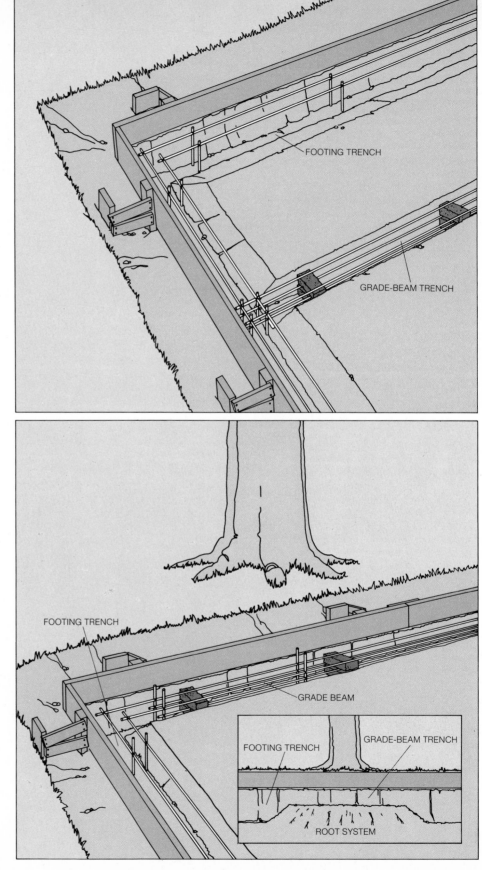

FOOTING TRENCH

GRADE-BEAM TRENCH

FOOTING TRENCH

GRADE BEAM

FOOTING TRENCH

GRADE-BEAM TRENCH

ROOT SYSTEM

The Standard Brick: A Shifting Size

The logic of building with standardized bricks has been apparent for millennia. But brickmakers and bricklayers have never been able to decide what the standard should be. Even today there are more than 30 versions of the "standard common brick" available in the United States. Admittedly, the differences are only fractions of an inch and come partly from the fact that brickmaking, even in this high-technology age, is still a localized industry. Clay deposits are nearly everywhere, so bricks are, in effect, still made on site.

Early bricks, molded by hand 10,000 years ago in the Middle East, were shaped one by one to fit a certain space. The loaf-shaped bricks were easily trimmed to fit, since they were only sun-dried mud. Fired bricks, developed by the ancient Sumerians, were less easily altered. So standardization began.

Building customs, not law, dictated the brick dimensions. The heavy walls of Sumerian houses and fortresses were made with bricks 2 feet square and 2 to 3 inches thick. Bricklaying was a two-man job: While one laid the mortar—mud or natural asphalt—a second hefted the brick into place.

Weight and improvements in kiln techniques also became factors in determining brick size. Wet clay is heavy, and when brickmakers began to use gang molds, around 3000 B.C., a mold containing four or five smaller bricks turned out to be all a brickmaker could comfortably lift. And there was the discovery that smaller bricks fired more evenly and were less vulnerable to breakage than 2-foot-square bricks.

In time, transportation figured in the size of bricks. The monumental structures of the Babylonians, built around the 6th Century B.C., demanded a kind of mass production. Brickyards were established near supply sources; they produced standard sizes that made the bricks easier to stack and to deliver to building sites. But the Babylonians did make larger bricks for the foundation, smaller ones for the courses above.

This practice of graduating brick sizes continued well into Roman times. Archeologists have discovered that much

Colossal use of bricks. Arches constructed of bipedales, a standard 2-foot-square Roman brick, outline the portals of the Colosseum. Pedales, 1-foot-square bricks, serve for the massive abutments; triangular half pedales form the bristling face of the wall below.

early Roman building was based on a brick called the pedale, which was approximately 1 foot square and 1½ to 2 inches thick. A half pedale existed, in either triangular or rectangular form, as did a bipedale, 2 feet square.

In the later years of the Roman Empire, smaller bricks, closer in size to the common brick of today, dominated Roman building. The Romans found that a single person, with a brick in one hand and a trowel in the other, could build much faster than two people working in tandem. The small brick, which could be held between thumb and fingers, was ideally suited to this concept.

By the Renaissance, the Roman bricklaying method had spread throughout the rest of Europe. Flemish and English bricklayers were setting bricks in bond patterns similar to those used today *(pages 99-100)*, and there was even a standard brick, with a length equal to twice its width and three times its height. But it remained for Queen Elizabeth I of England to codify brick sizes into law. In 1571, in response to complaints from bricklayers that variations in brick size from brickyard to brickyard made their work difficult, Elizabeth set the size of a brick at 9 inches long, 4¼ inches wide and 2¼ inches high.

Although Elizabeth's decree was later nullified, it did have one lasting effect on building construction. Housing for workers at the time was traditionally built with fireplaces two bricks wide—about 19 inches with the mortar joint. Firewood was cut 16 inches long to fill the grate, and when lath was needed for building, the woodpile was the easiest place to get it. Thus the familiar framing measure still in use today, 16 inches from stud center to stud center, probably originated in one brief stab at brick standardization.

The size of bricks used by British builders has changed many times since Elizabeth's day, but only modestly, fluctuating between 8 and 9 inches in length and very little in its other dimensions. For a time, American brickyards followed suit, but the splitting of the colonies from the mother country led to independence in brick sizes as well. Today, the accepted size for a standard brick in the United States is 7⅝ by 3⅝ by 2¼ inches. Manufacturers use steel dies to maintain these dimensions. But worn-out dies and clay variations mean that masons must often alter mortar joints to bring bricks up to standard.

Molding a Concrete Wall in a Wooden Form

Building a wooden form for a poured-concrete wall requires the skills of a carpenter rather than a mason. The form, or mold, for the concrete is a set of parallel wall panels constructed in much the same way as a partition wall, except that the supporting elements—the studs and the plates—are placed against the outside surfaces of the panels, leaving the interior surfaces smooth.

The form is usually made in sections, for easy dismantling. The sections must be perfectly aligned and plumb, and corners must fit precisely. The walls of the form must be leakproof, to contain the liquid concrete, and strong enough to support the concrete until it hardens sufficiently to stand alone.

Strength, in fact, is the form's most crucial attribute, for wet concrete is extremely heavy. The concrete in a section of form 8 feet long, 8 feet tall and 8 inches thick, for example, weighs more than 3 tons and exerts an outward pressure against the bottoms of the form of more than 1,200 pounds per square foot.

Before any carpentry for the form can begin, the concrete wall itself must be designed. In areas where codes do not require reinforcing steel in concrete, you can design a wall or foundation yourself. If you are at all unsure of your design abilities, or if steel reinforcement must be used to satisfy local requirements, you should hire a professional. Only an architect or an engineer is qualified to do the complex load and stress calculations that are needed to specify a wall strong enough to suit your needs and then translate those specifications into a set of detailed blueprints.

The blueprints will indicate the thickness of the wall and the proper placement of openings for doors, windows, pockets for beams, and foundation vents. Where required, the blueprints will also show the internal web of steel reinforcing bar, called rebar. In addition, you or the architect or engineer must design a suitable footing for the wall, specifying its size and the rebar it too requires.

With your plans in hand, you can apply for a building permit (page 27), then excavate the site (pages 34-39) and pour the footing (pages 40-45). At that point, you are ready to build the form wall.

Start by trimming 4-by-8 plywood panels, ⅝ inch thick, to the height of the finished wall. For walls 4 to 8 feet tall, use the panels upright; for walls less than 4 feet tall, turn the panels sideways. The panels are stiffened with horizontal 2-by-4 plates, top and bottom, and vertical 2-by-4 studs placed at 2-foot intervals.

Wherever the wall turns a corner, special filler panels are used. Often these are narrower than full panels, since their function is to fill the remaining space in a wall. In addition, the placement of their end studs is often different. At an outside corner, for example, where a filler panel usually intersects with a full panel, the end stud of the filler panel must be inset several inches, so that the edge of the filler panel can overlap the end stud of the intersecting wall. Inside corners, however, are invariably made with two intersecting filler panels, only one of which needs to have an inset stud.

Although it is possible to calculate the need for filler panels in advance of constructing the form wall, it is best not to cut them until the adjoining panels are in place. That way, you can measure exactly the space they have to fill.

After the prefabricated panels are built, they are joined together with hardware made specifically for concrete work. Central to the job are strong steel rods called wall ties (inset, opposite), which connect facing panels and are specially designed to perform two opposite functions. While the concrete is being poured, they hold the panels the proper distance apart. Then, when the wet concrete is in place, they hold the panels together, resisting the outward pressure of the concrete.

The wall ties slide through holes in the panels and project several inches beyond them. Eventually these projections are broken off, just below the surface of the concrete, leaving the center portion of the ties embedded within the finished wall. Scored lines, known as breakbacks, encircle the wall ties to make them easier to break.

Just outside the breakbacks, the wall ties are fitted with spacer washers, which hold the two form walls apart. Beyond the spacer washers, at the ends of the ties, are locking mechanisms that slip

over the ties to hold 2-by-4 horizontal braces, called wales, against the outside of the form, to keep it from collapsing under the weight of the concrete.

Although the design of wall ties may vary a bit from one manufacturer to another, the locking mechanism generally consists of a U-shaped bracket wide and deep enough to accept two wales. The arms of the bracket are pierced by two holes that slide over the wall tie and by a hole-and-pin arrangement that anchors the wales in place.

In the course of assembling the form walls, various internal elements must be added, including the rebar and wood or foam-plastic blockouts. Corresponding in size to the doors, windows and other openings, blockouts prevent the concrete from flowing into these areas. Additional blockouts can also be used to stop the flow of concrete between sections of wall, so that the entire wall need not be poured at once.

To get these internal elements in exactly the right position, it is necessary to assemble the form walls in a certain sequence. First the panels for the outside of the wall are raised and temporarily braced with buttresses while wall ties are inserted and wales are put in place. Next the blockouts are installed and the vertical rebar is hung from temporary spacer blocks at the top of the panels. Horizontal rebar is then laid across the ties and lashed to them, and to the vertical rebar, with 15-gauge steel wire. Finally the panels for the inside of the wall are set in place and secured with wales.

Once the form is completed, it must be inspected by the local building department. To pour without official approval of form construction is not only dangerous but may result in the imposition of a fine. In extreme cases, you could even be forced to take down the wall. If possible, set up an appointment for the form inspection in advance, in order not to delay the pour. Meanwhile, make your own final inspection. Check to make certain that all the pieces of rebar and all the blockouts are in the right positions and that all the walls are plumb.

Finally, just before the concrete is delivered, pack wet sand into the spaces between the panels and the footing.

A Structure Built for Stress

Forms for a foundation wall. A section of form for a house foundation—here unrealistically isolated from the rest of the wall for clarity—stands ready to receive the poured concrete. The form rests on a footing that has been notched, or keyed, lengthwise down the center *(page 45)* to help the wall resist lateral stresses. Each form panel is made of ⅝-inch plywood nailed to 2-by-4 framing consisting of a sole plate, a top plate and studs. The panels are linked to each other by wall ties *(inset)* inserted crosswise through the panels through holes cut or drilled at 2-foot intervals. Shallow grooves in the ties—called breakbacks—will allow the protruding ends of the ties to be snapped off after the concrete has set. Spacer washers on the ties hold the panels apart; U-shaped brackets and pins slip over the ends of the ties to anchor horizontal 2-by-4 wales, or braces, against the outside of the form. The panels are further braced, and are held plumb, by diagonal buttresses.

Positioned along the top of the panels at regular intervals, temporary spacer blocks hold the anchor bolts to which the 2-by-8 house sill will ultimately be attached. Other spacer blocks provide support for the steel wires from which the vertical rebar is hung. Horizontal rebar rests on the wall ties and is lashed to the ties and the vertical rebar with steel wire. A rectangular blockout, made of plastic foam and fastened to the panels with 16-penny (3½-inch) nails and adhesive, will prevent concrete from flowing into an area reserved for a wooden beam.

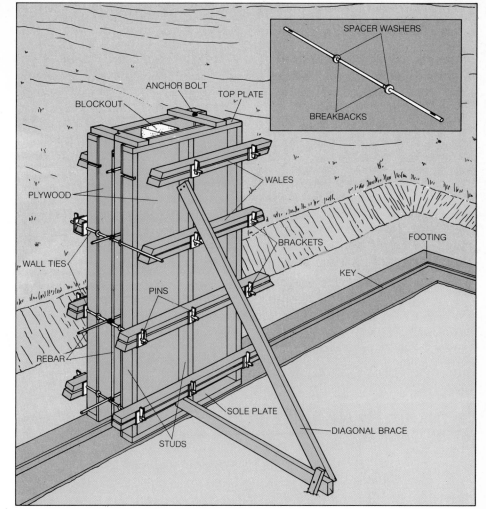

Constructing the Panels

Assembling panels. Using 2-by-4s, assemble a frame for each panel needed for the wall; here the plans call for a concrete wall 8 feet tall, so the frames are constructed to fit full 4-by-8 sheets of plywood. Nail the plywood to the frame. Starting 8 inches from the bottom of the panel, cut notches in the two outside studs at 2-foot intervals, making the notches half as deep as the diameter of the wall ties. To cut the notches, use a router or a circular saw, cleaning out wood scraps with a chisel. Drill holes alongside the inside stud at the same intervals.

When you need filler panels for the corners, rip the plywood to size, allowing for an extra 3½ inches to overlap the end stud of the adjacent panel. Assemble a frame, but position the corner stud to fall 3½ inches in from the edge of the panel. Nail the plywood to the frame, but put off drilling holes along the corner stud until the filler panel has been installed.

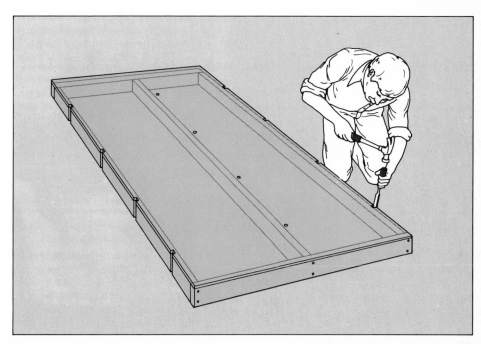

Oiling the forms. Coat the interior surface of the panels with a release agent, such as a light-grade motor oil, to prevent the concrete from sticking to the wood. Spray it on with a pressurized garden sprayer, applying the oil in a sweeping motion, in a thin, even coat. Wipe off any excess with a clean rag.

Used crankcase oil, which is less expensive than new oil, can also be applied as a release agent. It will stain the concrete, however, so it should be used only when the concrete will later be covered with paneling or wallboard.

Erecting the Panels for the Outside

1 **Connecting the panels.** Snap a chalk line on the footing to locate the outside edge of the concrete wall. Beginning at a corner, raise one panel into place, aligning its inside bottom edge with the chalk line. Have a helper raise a second panel into place, and butt it against the first. Check to make sure the plywood sheathing of the two panels is perfectly aligned and that the notches for the wall ties match. Nail the panels together through their studs, using 16-penny double-headed nails so that the panels can be easily dismantled after the concrete sets. Build a filler panel and use it to complete the run of the outside wall at the corner (inset).

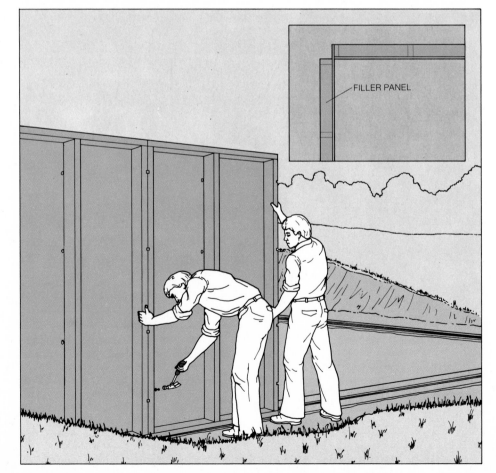

FILLER PANEL

2 **Plumbing the panels.** Drive a sturdy stake into the ground about 7 feet out from the joint between two panels, and lay a horizontal 2-by-4 brace between the stake and the joint. After checking to make sure the panel is flush with the chalk line, nail the brace first to the joint, then to the stake; place a sledge hammer behind the stake to steady it for nailing. Then, while a helper checks the panel for plumb with a carpenter's or mason's level, nail a diagonal 2-by-4 brace between the stake and the joint, at a point about 1 foot below the top of the panels.

Continue erecting panels along the chalk line; brace them every 8 feet to keep them plumb.

3 **Attaching wall ties and wales.** Push one end of each wall tie through the panels from the inside, until the spacer washers hit the plywood. Slip a U-shaped bracket over the projecting end of each tie, and drop a pin into the hole in the end of the tie to hold the bracket in place. Slide a wale through the brackets, resting it against the bottoms of the brackets. Then lay a second wale on top of the first, resting it on the ties. If wales must be butted end to end in order to span the wall, be sure to stagger the joints in the top and bottom wales (inset).

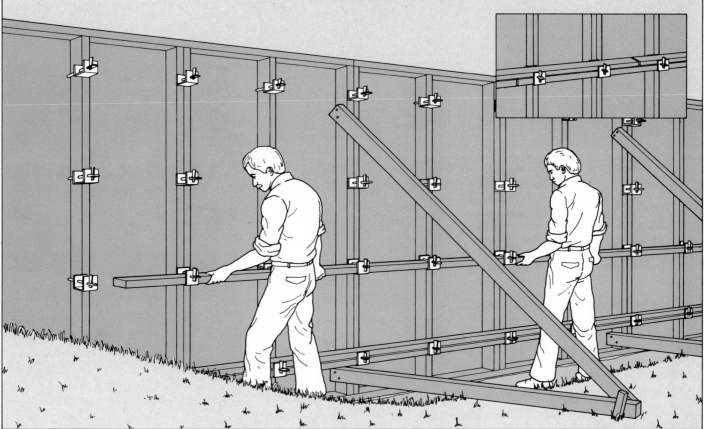

A Reinforcing Web of Steel

1 Hanging vertical rebar. To suspend rebar within the wall cavity, drive a double-headed nail into the center of a block of 2-by-4 scrap lumber 10 to 16 inches long. Nail this spacer block to the top of the panel, positioning it so that one long edge of the block lines up with a vertical row of wall ties and so that the center nail falls at what will be roughly the midpoint of the finished wall. In this 8-inch-thick wall, the center nail is located 4 inches from the inside face of the panel.

Prepare and mount similar spacer blocks at every location where the blueprints call for vertical rebar. Then cut sections of rebar long enough to reach from the bottom of the channeled key in the footing *(page 45)* to within 3 inches of the top of the panel. At each block, stand rebar in the key; hold the rebar upright by tying it to the center nail in the spacer block, using 15-gauge wire.

2 Tying horizontal rebar. At every height specified by the blueprints, rest a length of horizontal rebar on the wall ties to fall at the midpoint of the finished wall—in this instance, 4 inches from the inside face of the panel. Using 15-gauge wire, lash the horizontal rebar to the ties and to the vertical rebar wherever the rods cross.

At corners, bend a length of horizontal rebar as shown on page 43, center, and lap it at least 30 inches over the straight sections of rebar *(inset)*. Tie the overlapping rods together with wire in at least three places. Similarly, where straight runs of rebar must be joined together, overlap them approximately 30 inches, and tie them together in three places.

Blocking Out a Space for a Door or Window Opening

1 **Installing the frame.** Mark the location of the opening on the form wall, as specified by the blueprints, and construct a frame to fit around the opening. Use 2-inch-thick lumber, cut to fit the thickness of the finished wall so that, after the concrete is poured, the frame can be left in place as rough framing for the door or window. Cut the two sidepieces to fit the height of the opening, and cut a header to span them; for a window, cut a sill the same length as the header.

Add a key to the outside of each sidepiece, as anchors for the concrete. Construct the keys from strips of 1-by-4 lumber making them long enough to reach to the top of the header. Bevel both edges of the keys, and nail them to the center of the sidepieces (*inset*). Then mount the blockout on the wall, holding it against the opening while a helper nails it in place.

2 **Inserting spreaders.** To brace the blockout, cut spreaders to fit between the sidepieces at 2-foot intervals; make the spreaders from the same lumber used for the frame. For a door, set the first spreader directly against the concrete footing, wedging it between the sidepieces; for a window blockout, the sill serves as the bottom spreader. Toenail the remaining spreaders into the sides of the frame.

Cut two pieces of rebar 4 feet wider than the width of the opening, and lay them on top of the header, extending 2 feet on either side (*inset*). Anchor the pieces of rebar to the top of the header with bent nails to keep them from being jostled as the concrete is poured.

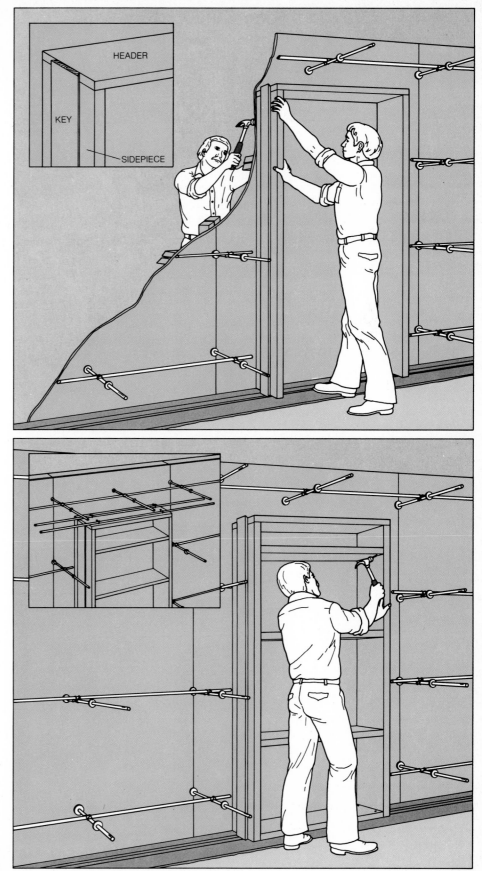

Creating Small Pockets for Vents and Floor Beams

Attaching a foam blockout. Mark the positions of any beams or vents on the inside of the form wall, using the blueprints as a guide. Drive several double-headed nails into the outlined areas from the outside of the form. Trace every opening on a block of polystyrene foam, the thickness of the concrete wall; cut out the foam blocks. Coat one face of each block with white glue or construction adhesive, and force the block onto the exposed nail points until it touches the form; the nails will hold the block in place until the adhesive sets. Do not pour the concrete directly onto the foam blockouts; the sudden weight could dislodge them.

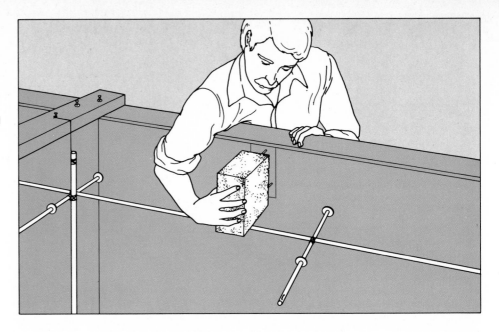

Completing the Form Walls

1 Erecting the inside walls. Snap a chalk line around the footing, marking the inside face of the completed concrete wall. Starting directly opposite a full-sized panel of the outside wall, raise a full-sized panel on the chalk line. Slide the panel over the free ends of the wall ties until it butts against the spacer washers. Then plumb the panel and secure it to the facing panel with a spacer block, nailed across the top plates.

Continue raising full-sized panels until only the inside corners of the form wall remain to be filled.

2 Making inside corners. At one side of each corner, measure the distance between the last full panel of one form wall and the chalk line marking the adjacent wall. Build a filler panel the right size to fill the space, offsetting the corner stud about 4 inches from the edge of the panel. Do not drill holes for wall ties along this corner stud. Erect the filler panel and secure it to the outside form wall with spacer blocks. Measure and build a second filler panel to fit the remaining space on the adjacent wall. Set this panel's corner stud directly against the panel edge, but do not notch the edge. Then slide the second panel into place, positioning it so that the corner studs will interlock as shown in the inset.

Drill holes for a row of wall ties linking the inside and outside corner panels, placing the holes within 2 feet of the outside corner. To align the holes, use the base of the panels and the edges of the nearest full panels as reference points. Insert ties through all the holes; if necessary, remove the spacer blocks and swing out the panels to fit the ties inside the wall cavity.

Complete the inside wall by sliding U-shaped brackets over the inside ends of the wall ties. Secure the brackets and add wales as in Step 3, page 55. With a level, check the wall for plumb, adjusting it, if necessary, by shifting the diagonal braces on the outside form wall.

Sectioning or Ending a Wall

Building a bulkhead. To stop the flow of concrete along a wall—either to end a wall in mid-run or to stop the pouring temporarily in order to reuse the form panels—you can install a special kind of blockout, known as a bulkhead. Although a bulkhead is set into position after the form walls have been completed, its use necessitates small changes at almost every stage of the form-building process. First, extend the last form panels before the bulkhead about 1 foot beyond the bulkhead location, so that the bulkhead can be recessed into the wall. Then, for a wall that is to be poured in sections and will later continue in a straight line, extend the horizontal rebar at least 30 inches past the location of the bulkhead so that it will overlap the rebar of the next section to be poured. For a wall that is to terminate at the bulkhead, cut the rebar 3 inches short of the bulkhead.

When all the lengths of rebar and all the form walls are in place, build and oil the bulkhead. It should be made of 2-inch-thick lumber, cut to the height and width of the finished wall. For a wall that is to continue, attach a beveled board to the inner surface of the bulkhead to create a key, as for the key on a footing (page 45, bottom); then drill holes in the bulkhead to accept the rebar. Slip the bulkhead into position, fastening it to the form walls with cleats. For a wall that is going to end at the bulkhead, simply omit the rebar holes and the key.

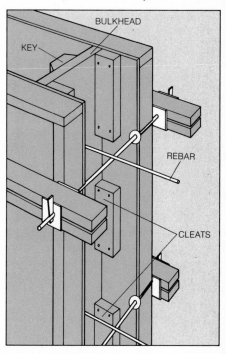

3 Suspending anchor bolts. Install anchor bolts for the sill at 6-foot intervals all around the form, hanging them from additional spacer blocks laid across the top plates. To do this, first drill a hole through the center of each block, slightly larger than the diameter of the bolt; this will allow you to wiggle the bolt in the wet concrete to dislodge any air bubbles. Slide the threaded end of the bolt through the hole, and fasten it against the block with a washer and nut. Then, using double-headed nails, anchor the block to the top plates.

After the form wall has been inspected, and just before the concrete is delivered, pack wet sand into the joint between the bottom of the plywood form and the footing.

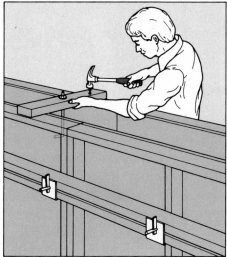

How to Orchestrate the Concrete Pour

Although the form work for a concrete wall can be done at a leisurely pace, once the concrete arrives everything must move like clockwork. The best way to ensure that this will happen is to draw up a battle plan and to call in extra troops—helpers to pitch in when the action starts.

A day or so before the pour, call the concrete supplier and arrange a delivery time that suits everyone involved. The company will need to know how many cubic yards of concrete you need and whether there are special requirements. For example, exterior walls usually require air-entrained concrete (page 40), but the degree of air entrainment may vary from 6 per cent in areas with severe climates to 4 per cent in milder ones.

Ready access to the concrete is essential for an efficient pour. On level sites that have not been landscaped, clear a space around the form walls so that the transit-mix truck can drive right in. If access to the walls is blocked by gullies or boulders, concrete can be fed to the site through an extension chute designed to cover distances up to 24 feet from the truck. If you need such a chute, inform the transit-mix company, since the chute that normally accompanies the truck is only 10 to 12 feet long.

Having a transit-mix truck drive onto a steep or landscaped site is not usually feasible. Because a fully loaded truck weighs more than 27 tons, it cannot maneuver on hills, and it might sink axle-deep in a lawn or crack a driveway. To get concrete to such sites, you will need a crane or a concrete pump—either of which can be rented from heavy-equipment rental agencies. The agency will arrange for a skilled operator to accompany the crane or the pump.

Pouring concrete with a crane presents no special problems. The operator will position the crane in such a way that the boom can swing between the transit-mix truck and the forms, carrying the concrete in a drop bucket.

A concrete pump, though a less elaborate piece of equipment, requires two people to handle the heavy, concrete-filled hose that runs from the pump to the form walls—one to direct the flow from the hose end, the other to keep the hose relatively straight. If it kinks, pressure will build, possibly bursting the hose with dangerous force.

If you use a pump, you must order concrete made with small, pea gravel in place of the usual limestone aggregate, which could clog the hose. You must also prepare a place to purge the hose of its contents whenever you interrupt the pour. One way is to set up forms for a driveway or porch steps and pump excess material into them. The hardened mass, a substitute for rubble, can later be covered by a smooth finish layer of concrete. Or simply purge the hose into a pit at the base of the wall, to be backfilled along with the footing.

When the preparations are complete and the concrete starts flowing, you must keep it moving evenly around the entire form. The mixture is extremely heavy and, if allowed to fill only one section of an 8-foot-tall form, could burst it. Instead, fill all of the forms, working continuously around the structure, in layers about 12 inches deep. This gives each layer time to set up slightly, providing support for the following layers.

As the concrete fills the forms, you will need at least three people to distribute it and free it of large air bubbles. Station one person at the point where the concrete enters the form to keep the chute, the pump hose or the drop bucket from overshooting its mark. A second worker, equipped with a length of rebar or a spade, should tamp the newly poured mass, forcing large pieces of aggregate away from the form wall and releasing air bubbles. Meanwhile, the third person should circulate around the walls, banging on them repeatedly with a rubber mallet, to prevent freed bubbles from clinging to the wall and creating a honeycomb pattern on the concrete surface.

After all of the concrete is poured, the top of the wall must be finished. First wiggle each anchor bolt to dislodge any air bubbles collected on it. Then trowel the top lightly to seal the surface. If a wood sill plate is to be attached, this is all the finish the concrete needs. However, if you intend to build a masonry wall above the concrete—or leave the wall top bare—give the top a second troweling (page 45). Finally, round the edges of the concrete with a corner trowel to prevent them from chipping when the forms are removed.

Concrete contractors sometimes remove the forms on the day after the pour, but it is better to wait three days to ensure that the wall has set properly. In dry weather, mist the wall top lightly with a garden hose every four hours for the first day; if rain is expected any time during the first 24 hours, cover the wall top with plastic sheets. Thereafter, expose it to the weather.

The task of stripping the form walls requires none of the precision used in erecting them. To dismantle the units, simply reverse the procedure you followed to build them. Remove the pins, wales and brackets. Pull the panels away from the wall and off of the ends of the wall ties. If a panel sticks to the concrete, a sharp blow with a mallet should dislodge it. If you must pull a panel away, wedge a pry bar behind it and loosen it gently to avoid chipping the wall. Snap off the wall ties with a hammer blow, or twist them off with large pliers. Finally, knock apart the panels themselves, pulling the nails carefully with a pry bar so that the lumber can be reused.

Pouring from a chute. With the transit-mix truck pulled as close to the form as possible, swing the chute into pouring position and signal the driver to start the flow of concrete. Use a plywood backstop to direct the flow, and keep the chute in motion to distribute the concrete evenly. When one section of wall is 12 inches deep, have the driver stop the flow of concrete and move the truck; change its location as often as necessary to pour all of the concrete in 12-inch layers.

As the concrete flows into the forms, have a second worker tamp it to release any air bubbles. For the first few layers, use a 10-foot length of rebar to tamp. As the level of the concrete rises to within reach, switch to a spade. In addition, slide the rebar or spade up and down repeatedly along the inside surfaces of the forms to keep air bubbles from collecting on them. Meanwhile, a third worker should be tapping all over the form walls with a rubber mallet.

Pouring with a pump. Have the transit-mix truck park on the street at a convenient place for the pump operator to set up the equipment—a pump at the base of the chute and enough 20-foot sections of hose to reach to every part of the form. Position one helper about 10 feet away from the form, to keep the heavy hose from kinking and to operate a remote on/off switch connected to the pump. This helper must watch the pouring operation carefully. If you drop the hose, or if you must take a short break to move a ladder, the helper will be able to shut off the machinery quickly. If you intend to take a break any longer than five minutes, be sure to in-form the pump operator, who will need to purge the pump and the hose.

Follow the same procedures as in pouring from a chute: Pour the concrete in 12-inch layers, and have two helpers control air bubbles by tamping the concrete and banging on the form.

Stopping Water

A masonry foundation must not only bear tremendous vertical loads, it must also be able to resist the intrusion of water from the surrounding soil. Depending on the amount of rainfall in a particular area, local building codes may call for one or more of the precautionary measures shown here.

The most common first step to take in keeping water in its place is to seal the joint between the walls and the footings with fresh mortar smoothed to a convex shape, known as a cove. If the walls are made of concrete block, additional mortar should be extended as a protective coating to above ground level.

A further step—taken only after the cove and any additional mortar are in place—is to coat the walls with a bituminous compound, made from either coal tar or asphalt. Such compounds are available at building-supply stores. To reinforce this layer, some building codes require a waterproof sheeting, called a membrane by professionals, to be pressed into the coating. The membrane can be roofing felt (a coarse, asphalt-impregnated paper), construction-grade polyethylene (black is preferable) or a more expensive plastic film.

Another aid in dealing with dampness is to lay drain tile around the foundation; the tile will carry water to a storm sewer, seepage area or some other disposal system. The tile—actually concrete or plastic pipe—can be perforated or unperforated, but it should be at least 4 inches in diameter. Unperforated tile must be laid with a 1-inch gap between lengths to let water enter the pipe and drain away.

If a bituminous compound or a plastic membrane has been applied to the foundation, it is good practice, and sometimes a requirement, to cover the coatings or membrane with styrofoam board—or even roofing felt—before backfilling. This protective covering prevents any sharp stones in the dirt from puncturing the waterproof layers. Such damage could occur either when the backfill is pushed against the foundation or when changes in temperature shift the soil.

Moistureproof Coatings to Protect the Wall

1 **Troweling on the cove.** Dampen the exposed horizontal part of the footing. If the wall is of poured concrete, dampen the vertical surface of the joint to a height equal to the exposed footing's width. Using the same mortar mixture as for joining concrete block (*page 74*), trowel on enough mortar to cover the dampened portions of the footing and wall. Shape the mortar into a rounded cove.

If the wall is of concrete block, dampen the entire wall to about 6 inches above the eventual ground level; after you have troweled on the cove, continue to cover the wall with a coat of mortar about ⅜ inch thick; the coating should be slightly thicker at the bottom. Roughen the mortar with a leaf rake or a trowel; after 24 hours, add a second coat, equally thick.

2 **Adding a bituminous coating.** After the wall has cured (about 3 dry days for a mortar-covered block wall, 14 days for a poured-concrete wall), use a brush, roller or trowel to apply two layers of bituminous coating over the mortar coating applied in Step 1. The coating can be either coal tar or asphalt, but do not mix the two. Extend the coating from the bottom of the cove to ground level.

3 Pressing on an impervious membrane. For extra protection in wet areas, cut waterproof membrane—either polyethylene or roofing felt—to fit between the footing and the top of the bituminous coating. Press the membrane into the bituminous coating while the coating is still pliant—within one or two hours. If you use a polyethylene membrane, apply it vertically as shown at right, overlapping the seams 8 inches. Seal the seams with the bonding agent recommended by the membrane manufacturer. Roofing felt should be applied horizontally in overlapping courses, beginning at the bottom of the mortared cove. Each succeeding course should overlap the one below by about 6 inches. Seal the seams with bituminous coating compound. Whichever membrane you use, wrap it around wall corners by at least 2 feet.

Where dampness is a severe problem—if a house is built into a hillside, for example—use membrane made of butyl or of ethylene propylene diene, which are more expensive but more effective. Both kinds of membrane are available from building-supply stores.

A Drain to Carry Away Ground Water

Laying the drain tile. In the excavation around the footing, tamp out a 6-inch-wide border to lay the tile on. Grade the border in a gentle slope leading to a trench that runs to a storm sewer, dry well or seepage area downhill. Make the slope 1 inch in 12 feet, starting at the point farthest from the drainage trench. Lay the tile against the footing and, if none is already there, in the trench that leads to the drainage area.

Leave 1-inch gaps between tile sections (the gaps are essential with unperforated tile; they save time and materials if the tile is perforated). Put two layers of roofing felt over joints (*right*) to keep out silt. With tile perforated in one line of slots, face the slots away from the wall.

Add 6 to 8 inches of coarse gravel, then add roofing felt or polyethylene to keep silt out. Backfill carefully—first with a shovel, then with a backhoe, if you can get one. Tamp the soil after the addition of each vertical foot of backfill.

If you have used a trench to form the mold for the footing—and if local codes permit—lay the tile at ground level against the cove (*inset*). Then follow the procedures above.

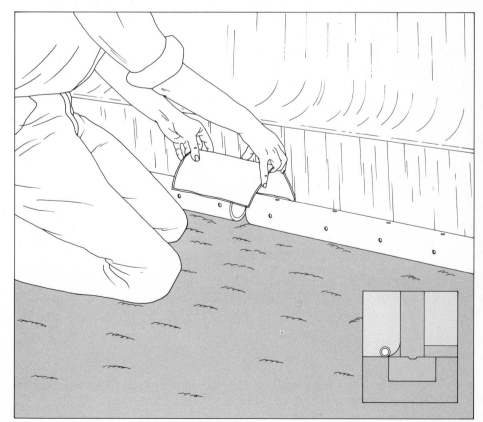

Casting Concrete into Decorative Blocks

In addition to its role in walls and slabs cast as a single piece, poured concrete can be used to create individual concrete blocks in a variety of shapes, colors and textures. Especially appropriate for decorative structures such as garden walkways, low walls and borders for flower beds, these ornamental blocks are usually cast in removable wooden forms, although the concrete is sometimes poured directly into cavities scooped out of the earth *(opposite)*.

Wooden forms for ornamental blocks are made of smooth lumber and are set over a plywood base, which can be covered with building paper, form oil, or polyethylene film to prevent the concrete from sticking. For easy removal, the forms are hinged; if several blocks are to be cast at once, the forms can be built in gridlike gangs.

The forms are oiled and the concrete is poured, packed, and leveled in much the same way as for a concrete footing *(pages 40-45)*. But the quantities of concrete involved are much smaller. You can mix the concrete yourself in a wheelbarrow or a mortar pan, adding water to premixed concrete or to a basic mix of one part cement, two parts sand and three parts coarse aggregate.

One way to give pattern and texture to handmade blocks is to line the forms with such materials as ridged rubber matting, polyethylene or strips of wood. However, be careful not to use a lining material with an undercut pattern that might interfere with removing the block from the mold. And in climates where alternate freezing and thawing occur, do not use patterns that act to collect rain; the expansion and contraction of trapped water would crumble the block's surface. So that the concrete can flow into the crevices in the form liner, use aggregate no more than ¼ inch in diameter.

Many standard concrete mixtures produce surfaces that are decorative in themselves. Portland cement can be acquired in white as well as the usual beige, for example, and many suppliers offer alternate choices of yellow, brown or white sand. In addition, there are decorative aggregates, such as polished pebbles and marble chips, that create interesting built-in textures.

Other decorative surfaces can be produced by roughening the concrete. In one technique the surface of the block is layered to resemble travertine *(page 67)*; in another it is pocked with salt crystals that subsequently dissolve *(page 67)*. But since both these textures create rain traps, they should not be used where freezing and thawing are common.

Color is added in the form of mineral-oxide pigments. Precolored cement to use in the concrete mixture is available at building-supply stores. However, it is cheaper to add pigment to the cement yourself—and the color choice is wider. Mineral oxides come in every basic color, and they can be mixed together to create a wide variety of other hues. To achieve the clearest colors possible, use white cement, white sand and white aggregate.

Colored concrete should be mixed only in an automatic mixer, never by hand; otherwise the results will be blotchy. Put the pigment in the mixer along with the cement and the aggregate, and blend them until the color is uniform. Then add water as usual. The strength of the color will, of course, depend on the proportion of pigment to cement. For a pastel color, the usual proportions are 1 or 2 pounds of pigment to every 100 pounds of cement; for deep shades, a good ratio is 7 pounds of pigment to every 100 pounds of cement.

Always measure the ingredients by weight rather than volume, and never add more than 10 per cent pigment, lest you weaken the concrete. If you are uncertain about the exact color you want, make several small test batches, adding varying amounts or combinations of pigment to the dry mixture before putting in the water. Then allow these miniature blocks to cure for about a week; their color will change slightly in curing. Be sure to keep a record of the ingredients for each batch, so that you can duplicate the chosen color exactly.

When adding either color or decorative aggregate, one way to economize is to cast the blocks in two layers, using pigment or aggregate in the top layer only. In making these tiered blocks, fill the form to within an inch of the top with ordinary concrete. Add the second layer, containing the pigment or aggregate, when the first layer is stiff enough to support it.

Another cost-saving alternative in using aggregate is to press the aggregate into the top of the concrete block *(page 67)*. And the most economical way to apply color is with a mixture called dry-shake—a combination of pigment, cement and sand that is sprinkled on top of the still-damp concrete block and floated in. You will need a pound of dry-shake for every 2 square feet of concrete. To get the colored layer even, first sift about two thirds of the mixture through your fingers onto the floated concrete surface. After several minutes, when the dry-shake mixture has absorbed some moisture from the concrete, smooth it with a float. Then sift on the rest of the dry-shake and trowel the surface smooth.

Molds for Blocks from Earth and Wood

Earth forms for steppingstones. Working on site, dig holes 3 inches deep in the shapes of the blocks. Cut the edges with a spade or a garden trowel so that the perimeters are clean and as nearly vertical as possible. Pour and finish each steppingstone individually. Fill the hole with concrete, then tamp and smooth it with a wood float, leaving the stone with a slightly rough but uniform texture.

When you are setting concrete steppingstones into a lawn, as shown here, it is best to make their top surface level with the surrounding earth, so that they will not interfere with convenient operation of the lawn mower.

Wood forms for single blocks. Cut four pieces of smooth lumber for a frame. Miter and hinge one frame corner. Butt-join the two adjacent corners; close the fourth with a hook and eye.

Set the frame on plywood; coat the plywood and frame with form oil. Fill the form, then tamp and level the concrete with a 2-by-4. Run a trowel between the concrete and the form to compact the edges, then trowel the surface smooth. After 10 minutes, remove the frame, wash it with water, and repeat the process. Let the blocks cure for four days before moving them.

To make interlocking blocks, add removable inserts to a square frame: L-shaped pieces for a cruciform block; mitered corner pieces for a hexagon (inset). For the blocks to fit together, all sides of the form must be the same length.

Ganged forms for mass production. To cast multiple paving blocks on site, construct a rectangular frame of 2-by-3s. Assemble the frame so that its long sides extend 1 inch beyond each end, and nail 1-by-2s between the end extensions to make handles. Install 2-by-3 dividers inside the frame to define compartments of the desired shapes. Oil the form, cast the concrete and cure the blocks as for an individual form (above, right), but screed all the blocks at once by pulling a 2-by-4 over their surface. Wait at least 15 minutes before removing the form. Reposition it and repeat the process.

To cast multiple building blocks, make a demountable grid of smooth lumber notched at intervals to half its width so that the notches interlock. Position the notches to create the block shapes desired. Oil the form sections before putting them together, and set the assembled form on oiled plywood. Cast the blocks as described above. Wait 15 to 20 minutes before disassembling the form, then allow the blocks to cure for a week before using them.

Creating Patterns with Form Liners

Rubber matting. To model the surface of a concrete block with diagonal ridges, use skidproof rubber matting, normally sold for doormats and stair treads. Dip the matting in water and place it in the bottom of an oiled form. Pour in a relatively wet mix of concrete, then tamp, level and cure the blocks as on page 65.

Embossing with gravel. To produce the dimpled surface shown at right, place a sheet of household plastic wrap or other polyethylene film over a bed of smooth gravel. Use gravel of fairly uniform size and distribute it evenly over an area that matches the internal dimensions of the form, leaving spaces between the individual stones. Then lay the film loosely over the gravel so that the weight of the concrete will force the film into the spaces. Position the oiled form over the plastic, and pour and finish the concrete as described on page 65.

Wood strips. To create a pattern of ridges and grooves, position strips of wood in the bottom of the form. The edges of the wood strips should be beveled slightly; otherwise they may stick in the concrete. In the example at right, the ridges in the finished block were roughened with a cold chisel and a maul. To cast variations, use half-round or triangular molding, or arrange the wood strips in a square. Coat the strips with form oil before positioning them on the oiled base, and use concrete somewhat wetter than usual. Tamp it well to be sure that it will flow into the gaps between the strips.

Wood-block dies. To add light and shadow to a plain concrete-block wall, intersperse blocks patterned with geometric bas reliefs created with wood-block dies. In this example, triangular dies are placed in the corners of the oiled form to form dramatic trapezoid shapes. When using dies with exposed end grain, be sure to sand the end grain smooth so that the dies slip easily from the finished concrete blocks. If the pattern is raised, as here, deepen the form by the depth of the dies, to bring the recessed areas level with the surrounding wall. Oil the dies before inserting them in the form; then cast and finish the concrete as described on page 65.

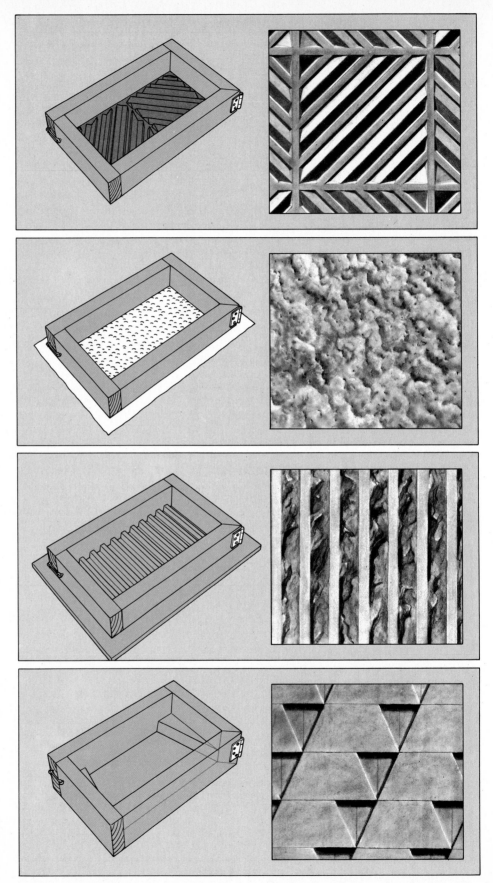

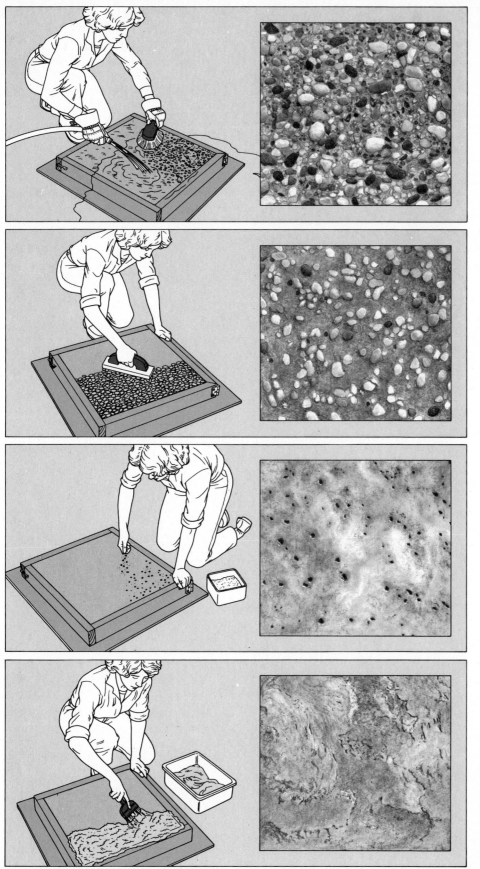

Roughened Surfaces for Textural Interest

Exposed aggregate. To bring decorative aggregate into relief, wash a thin layer of cement from the top of the block. First, finish the block through the troweling stage *(page 65)*, and let it set until the aggregate is firmly anchored but the cement is still soluble—about an hour. Then, with a garden hose and a stiff brush, simultaneously flush and scrub the top of the block until the top of the aggregate is exposed. Test a corner of the block first to see if brushing tends to dislodge the aggregate.

Pebbled paving. To add a veneer of pebbled paving to a plain concrete block, fill the oiled form with concrete to within ¼ inch of the top. Level the surface with a 2-by-4, notched ¼ inch deep at the ends to fit over the edges of the form. Then wet down the pebbles or stones of the aggregate, and distribute them in a single layer over the concrete. Press the aggregate into the concrete with a float until it is buried just below the surface. When the concrete is set but the cement is still soluble, flush and brush the surface as above to reveal the top of the aggregate.

A salt-pitted surface. To create a delicate pattern of pockmarks in concrete, scatter large grains of rock salt over the block while it is still damp—just after it has been floated or troweled smooth. Press the salt crystals into the concrete with a float, but do not bury them. Allow the block to cure, then wash away any undissolved salt with a garden hose.

A travertine finish. To add the rough, streaked look of travertine to concrete block, screed the surface to compact it, but float it only lightly, so that the concrete retains a rough surface. Then use a mason's utility brush to dab on mortar made of two parts cement to one part sand, coating the concrete with an uneven, patchy surface, with ridges up to ¼ inch high. When the water sheen disappears, float or trowel off the tops of the ridges, leaving both mortar and concrete rough in the crevices between. To heighten the streaked look, tint the mortar topping with mineral-oxide pigment *(page 64)* before you put it on the concrete.

Adobe Bricks Made from Stabilized Mud

Bricks of sun-dried mud have been a common building material for millennia, possessing the great advantage of requiring nothing more than earth, water and a strong back to make them. However, they are vulnerable to erosion by water and wind, a drawback that has been overcome by the modern practice of adding emulsified asphalt to the mud. This emulsion, used for paving roads, is available from oil dealers and paving contractors: Order emulsion SS-1h or equivalent.

Stabilized adobe bricks are a practical building material wherever the right soil is available and the climate is dry enough to cure them. Although impervious to rain showers after a few days, they require at least three weeks of dry weather to harden properly. Suitable adobe soil can be found not only in semidesert regions, such as the southwestern United States, but in any other area where the soil consists primarily of sand and clay; dark soil containing much organic matter will not cohere into bricks. A simple suitability test for soils is shown at right.

Traditionally, adobe structures were mortared together with the same mud that the bricks were made of. Adobe structures of stabilized bricks are assembled much like those of standard bricks, using mortar containing one part cement, two parts soil, three parts sand, and 1½ gallons of asphalt emulsion per 100 pounds of cement. Mortar joints for adobe bricks are thick—¾ inch—and the footing for the structure should extend above ground level.

The only way to establish conclusively whether your soil is suitable for adobe is to make test bricks of the dimensions planned for construction. If you plan to build a structure that is subject to code, bricks with the correct proportion of asphalt emulsion can be sent to a commercial laboratory to be tested for strength, absorption and moisture content.

Made in wood forms, adobe bricks are 4 inches thick but can vary in length and width according to local custom and intended use. A good size for a first job, a low wall or a hearth, is 4 by 10 by 14 inches. A brick this size will weigh approximately 30 pounds.

The keys to mixing adobe mud are to add the right amount of water and to remove every lump of clay. The mud must be soft enough to work but stiff enough not to slump more than ¼ inch when the forms are removed. In two or three days the test bricks will be dry enough to determine whether they will crack or crumble.

If the bricks crumble, the clay content is too low, and you will have to add clay or abandon the project. If they crack, the simplest remedy is to shade them as they dry. Or add straw, cut into roughly 4-inch lengths, to the mud. If neither remedy is successful, the clay content is probably too high, and you will have to add coarse builder's sand.

Bricks that are to be stabilized with emulsified asphalt also require preliminary tests to determine how much emulsion to add. Begin by making test batches, using ⅛ cubic foot of soil and adding a cup of emulsion in one batch, ¼ cup more and ¼ cup less in two others.

To mix the batches, measure the soil in a container whose interior forms a 6-inch cube. Transfer the soil to a bucket, mix in the water and the emulsion, and stir until the color is uniform. Shape the batches by hand into miniature bricks and allow them to dry—you can hasten this process by putting them in a 140° F. oven.

To be sure that the bricks are completely dry, break one in half. Then immerse the others in water for several hours. A well-waterproofed brick will not soften, even at the edges. Continue making test bricks with less and less emulsion until you arrive at the smallest amount that provides adequate waterproofing.

Mud for stabilized adobes must be mixed in a power-driven mortar mixer in order to distribute the emulsion evenly. Once you are satisfied with your test bricks, figure out how much emulsion is needed for 1 cubic foot of soil, then multiply by the capacity of your mixer. Mortar mixers in various cubic-foot capacities can be rented from construction-equipment companies. The mud for unstabilized adobe can be mixed with a shovel and a hoe in the pit created when the soil is excavated.

Analyzing the Soil Content

A water test for clay content. Collect a sample of the soil you plan to use. In some areas, suitable soil occurs at surface level; in others, you will need to dig below the layer of humus-rich topsoil. With a shovel, break and mix the soil to be tested and remove any large stones. Place several handfuls of soil in a quart jar, and add water to cover it by 3 or 4 inches. Cap the jar and shake it until the soil and water are thoroughly mixed.

When the soil has settled into layers, measure first the total height of the soil column, then the thickness of the smooth top layer of clay and silt, called fines. Divide the thickness of the layer of fines by the height of the soil column to determine the percentage of fines in the soil. It should be in the range of 25 to 45 per cent; the rest should be sand and small pebbles.

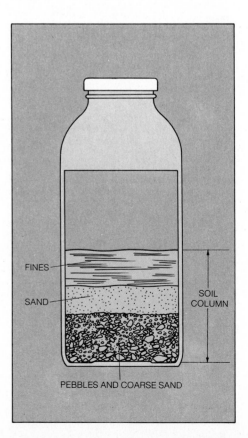

FINES

SAND

SOIL COLUMN

PEBBLES AND COARSE SAND

Mixing Adobe Mud

Using a mortar mixer. Pour a few inches of water into the mixer's hopper, then shovel in the soil. Add water to make a stiff mud. Turn on the mixer and let the paddles revolve until all lumps disappear; if you are using asphalt stabilizer, slowly add the required amount while the paddles are turning. Keep mixing until the mud is uniform in color and texture. To test the consistency, stop the mixer and groove the mud with your finger. The sides of the groove should bulge slightly but not run together.

If you are using straw, add about one part straw to five parts soil and mix again, but only until the straw is scattered throughout the mud; too much mixing can cause the straw to wrap around the paddles. When the mixture is ready, tilt the hopper, using the dump handle, and have a helper shovel the mud into a wheelbarrow.

To help break up clods of clay in the mud, prepare the soil for mixing the day before. Turn it over and mix it, remove any stones, then soak it with water. Cover the soil with plastic so that the water will be absorbed overnight.

Changing Mud into Bricks

Molding the bricks. For multiple bricks, construct a gridlike form consisting of a frame subdivided into compartments. Use smooth lumber 4¼ inches wide. Fasten the form together with screws and reinforce the corners with steel corner braces set into the wood. Screw wooden cleats to both ends to serve as handles.

To use the form, wet it thoroughly and place it on level ground covered with heavy brown paper or plywood. Tip the wheelbarrow and shovel the mud into the form, overfilling each compartment slightly. Then wet your hands and press down on the mud, spreading it to fill the corners of the compartments completely.

Finish the top of the bricks by pulling a wet 2-by-4 over the form edges. Lift off the form immediately, clean it well with water and a stiff brush, then repeat the procedure. Allow the bricks to dry flat until they are firm enough to hold their shape, one to four days depending on air temperature and humidity. Then stand them on edge to dry both faces. In three to six weeks, they will be ready for use or storage. Store unused bricks in rows slightly tilted against a central pillar of flat bricks.

A Strengthened-Earth Paving

Soil cement, an alternative to concrete paving, uses soil rather than sand and gravel as the filler material for the cement. Earth normally removed to make way for a concrete slab thus becomes part of the pavement. The resulting surface is less durable than concrete, but it is far easier and cheaper to achieve.

Soil cement looks more like soil than like concrete; it has a rough, often crackled finish and an earthen hue. Consequently, it is best used for informal walkways, as a subpavement for a brick or tile patio, or as an alternative to a dirt driveway or parking area. For foot traffic and subpavement, soil and cement are usually mixed to a depth of 4 inches; for a heavily used driveway or any surface subject to freezing and thawing, a depth of 6 inches is recommended.

The durability of soil cement depends on using the correct ratio of cement to soil, which in turn depends on the nature of the soil. The correct ratio of cement to soil ranges from 6 per cent for sandy, gravelly soils to as much as 20 per cent for soils with some organic matter. Some soils, such as those rich in clay or organic matter, are simply unsuitable.

To find the best proportions for your paving project, make test samples, using a kitchen measuring cup to vary the proportion of cement to soil and molding the moistened mixture in tin cans or muffin tins. Wrap the samples in plastic to cure for a week, then unmold them and soak them in water for four hours. After removing them, test the surface of each sample by striking it with the tip of a dull ice pick or awl or with the tip of a nail; the tool should penetrate no more than ¼ inch. Then rap each one sharply with a hammer; the sample that rings clearest contains the best mix.

To determine the total amount of cement you will need, multiply the percentage of cement in the best sample by the total volume of the job. For example, if the sample contains 10 per cent cement and you plan to cover a pathway 20 feet long and 3 feet wide with soil cement 4 inches deep, the total soil volume is 20 cubic feet, and the cement needed will be 2 cubic feet—or two 94-pound bags.

Correct timing is as important as a correct mixture. Since all soil contains some moisture, cement begins to hydrate, or set up, as soon as it is spread on the soil. Consequently, you must spread only as much cement as you can incorporate, moisten and compact in one work session. The simplest procedure is to prepare the entire site, then to divide it into sections, each containing the correct amount of soil for one bag of cement; the sections can be marked off either with lime or with string. Incorporate the cement section by section, mixing one bag at a time.

Although soil cement can be mixed and laid entirely by hand, two power tools speed the work. A rotary tiller can be used to pulverize the soil (*Step 1, below*) and incorporate the cement (*Step 2, opposite*). And a power tamper will compact the mixture of soil and cement much more quickly than hand tamping (*Step 4, opposite*).

Constructing a Durable Pathway

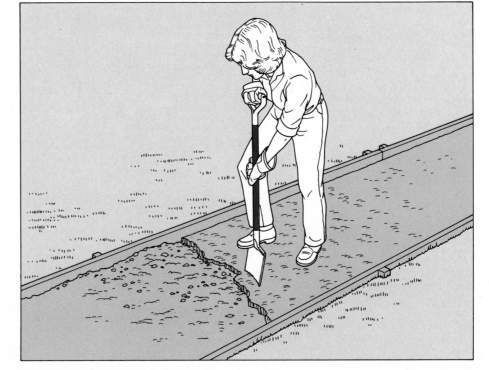

1 **Preparing the soil.** Remove any sod or topsoil covering the paving site. Brace the surrounding earth with boards and stakes, or create a permanent border of bricks. Use a shovel to turn over and pulverize the remaining soil to the planned depth of the paving, breaking up any large clods of dirt and removing any stones that are more than 1 inch in diameter. Smaller stones can be allowed to remain, to be incorporated later, when you mix the soil cement. Then rake the soil to form a smooth layer of uniform thickness.

2 **Incorporating the cement.** Working in sections, spread cement in an even layer over the soil, and work it in with a hoe until the mixture of soil and cement is a uniform color throughout the depth planned for paving. Check for uniformity by cutting through the mixture with a shovel. When it is uniform, rake the surface smooth.

3 **Adding water.** Moisten the surface of the soil-and-cement mixture, using a fine spray of water from a garden hose. Then work the water into the mixture to the full depth of the paving, using a hoe, as in Step 2. Test the mixture for its moisture content by squeezing a handful; it is sufficiently moist when the handful forms a ball that can be broken apart cleanly, without crumbling. Be careful that you do not add more water than necessary. When the moisture content is right, rake the surface smooth.

4 **Compacting the surface.** Pound the soil cement with a tamper—here, a 1-foot square of ¾-inch plywood with a braced handle of 2-by-4 lumber. Use enough force to compact the soil cement to its full depth. When the paving is evenly tamped, score it lightly with a rake to remove irregularities. Then pull a 2-by-4, the width of the paving, over the surface. Dampen the surface lightly a second time, with a garden hose, and tamp it once again, producing a surface as firm as hard-packed earth. For a very smooth finish, run a lawn roller or a tennis-court roller over the soil cement. Cure the soil cement as you would a concrete slab (*page 49*).

Walls of Brick, Block and Stone

Getting a handle on bricks. Easing the task of shifting bricks from storage pile to work site, a steel carrier compresses up to 10 bricks in a rigid stack. The carrier's two sliding sections are easily adjusted by a bolt, and the clawlike ends, loosely fitted around a row of bricks, clamp tight when the handle is lifted. Brick carriers, which are commonly used by professionals, can be rented from tool suppliers.

However imposing the finished structure, a building made of bricks, blocks or stone rises in manageable increments, on a comfortably human scale. Walls of almost limitless bulk and weight are composed of masonry units that a single worker can lift, and they are bonded together with mortar, a concoction so prosaic that masons often call it mud. Even the skills essential to masonry are simple: One twist of the wrist spreads mortar in an even bed, another twist butters an individual component and a third settles it into place.

But if individual bricks, blocks and stones are simple to heft and mortar together, no one should underestimate their balkiness and complexity en masse. A single brick is tractable; a 1-ton cube of 500 bricks, delivered at the front of a driveway for a building project in the backyard, poses a challenge equivalent to moving a small mountain. And although one brick laid slightly askew in a rising wall may pass unnoticed, the sum of many small misalignments is an unsightly and potentially unstable structure.

To ensure that the apparent simplicity of the work does not lead to pitfalls, advance planning is essential. For many masonry projects, the planning will inevitably involve a certain amount of paperwork. When brick or stone is being used to sheathe an existing wall, for example, every dimension of the new wall has to mimic the dimensions of the wall being covered—and this requirement often means that even the thickness of the mortar joints must be calculated ahead of time. For decorative brickwork, a sketch that charts the patterns and shifts of color will provide an invaluable guide to laying the bricks. And for an arch or a serpentine wall, you will have to employ some basic principles of geometry to design the curved plywood template against which the bricks will fit.

For any wall you must also settle in advance on a method for keeping the courses of masonry rising straight and true. In most cases this is done with corner leads built at opposite ends of a wall— several courses of brick or block that rise in stepped rows from ground level. The mason's line that is stretched between the leads guides the placement of all the intervening bricks.

Preliminary planning can also help you cope with the weight and volume of masonry materials. Before the bricks, blocks or stones arrive, set up a routine with your helper or helpers. Typically, professional masons arrange to have small caches of materials distributed along the wall they are erecting—piles of 40 to 50 bricks, or 8 to 10 blocks or stones, placed about 6 feet apart and about 2 feet back from the wall—with full boards of mortar interspersed between the piles. The mason is thus never out of reach of the supplies, which are kept constantly replenished by helpers.

Concrete Blocks for Modular Construction

Concrete blocks are the ideal building material for structures where ruggedness and low cost are of prime importance. In a basement, a foundation wall, or an entire new building, they provide more strength and durability for the amount of time and labor expended than virtually any other masonry material.

Contributing to the speed with which the blocks can be laid are their size and regularity. One standard concrete block occupies the same volume as 12 average bricks and requires far fewer mortar joints. And all blocks are based on a modular unit of 8 by 16 inches (the actual dimensions of each block are ⅜ inch shorter to allow for a mortar joint).

Standard blocks are available in thicknesses ranging from 4 to 12 inches; 8-inch blocks are most commonly used for foundations and structural walls. Check local building codes to find the thickness required in walls of the type you plan.

In addition, blocks come in configurations suiting them to various structural needs. For example, most walls, like those in the illustration on this page, are built with a combination of flush-ended and flange-ended blocks. The former are used at corners; the latter are stretcher blocks, used to fill in the remainder of the wall. Fractional blocks, including half units and 4-inch-thick partition blocks (so named because they are commonly used for internal walls) reduce the need for measuring and cutting blocks. And speed blocks, which have lateral cores, serve as conduits for the horizontal reinforcing bars.

To help make construction quicker, many structural materials are sized to match the dimensions of the blocks. Precast lintels, needed to support the weight of the wall over door and window openings, are available in widths that match the thickness of the blocks. Steel joint-reinforcement wire also comes in widths that conform to block widths.

In areas of the country that are susceptible to high winds or seismic activity, local codes may specify that walls contain vertical as well as horizontal reinforcement. For this, use a ½-inch diameter steel rebar *(page 40),* cut into 4- to 6-foot lengths to facilitate installation.

To determine the number of blocks you will need for a structure, multiply the length of the walls, in feet, by the number of courses. Multiply this result by ¾ to obtain the number of blocks required for a solid wall. Use the same formula to determine how many blocks to subtract for window and door openings, if any. Add 10 per cent to your final figure to allow for breakage—loose blocks chip easily and often crack when jostled.

Since individual blocks weigh between 25 and 35 pounds—and most projects require hundreds of blocks—it is important to have your order delivered as close to the work site as possible. Plan a storage area easily accessible to the delivery truck. An ideal spot is on level ground, about 6 feet inside the footing, to allow room for scaffolding. Cover the stored blocks with waterproof tarpaulins to keep them dry. Wet blocks expand slightly and, when they shrink on drying, may cause cracks in mortar joints.

Although you can buy mortar that is premixed, for most large jobs it is more economical to mix it on site, using clean sand and masonry cement. The correct mixture combines one part of cement with three parts of sand and enough water to give the mortar a mushy consistency—it should hold to the face of an inclined trowel until shaken off. Mortar mixed with one standard 94-pound bag of cement requires about 5 U.S. gallons of water; this yields 3 cubic feet of mortar, enough to lay about three dozen blocks. Buy 1 ton of sand for every eight bags of cement you need.

Mix the mortar with water in a mortar pan, using a mortar hoe. Mortar dries out and stiffens quickly—generally in one to two hours, although high temperature speeds the process and high humidity retards it. Prepare fresh mortar in small batches as you work, based on the rate at which you use it.

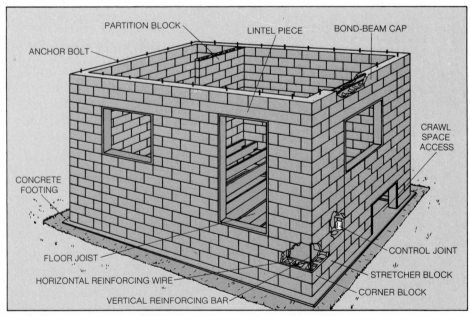

Anatomy of a concrete-block structure. This building's foundation wall rests on a poured-concrete footing. Vertical steel rebar reinforces the wall at corners and beside door and window openings. The horizontal joint of every second course has steel joint-reinforcement wire for lateral stability. Precast reinforced concrete lintels are used above door and window openings, and vertical control joints are placed near such openings to absorb expansion and contraction during temperature changes. Wood floor joists are set into wall pockets, and rough wood frames for doors and windows are added.

At the roof line, a bond-beam cap, composed of horizontal rebar embedded in mortar within the trough of a top course of speed block, adds lateral strength to the wall. The bond-beam cap also is the base for the 8-inch, L-shaped anchor bolts that tie the roof to the wall.

BUILDING LINES

MASON'S LINE

Laying the First Course

1 **Mortaring the footing.** After building a footing suitable for the planned wall *(pages 40-45)*, stretch strings between the batter boards to indicate the building lines. Using the lines as reference points, trowel a level bed of mortar at one corner. Make the mortar bed about 1½ inches thick and 2 inches wider than the thickness of the block, and spread it only far enough to reach an inch beyond the block.

Set the corner block in the mortar, allowing the weight of the block to compress the joint to a thickness of ⅜ inch. Then set another corner block at the other end of the building line.

2 **Leveling the corner blocks.** Rest a mason's level on each corner block, and tap the block with the handle of a trowel until the block rests flat on its mortar bed. Once two corner blocks are mortared and leveled, string a mason's line *(below)* along their outside faces; the mason's line will serve as a guide in aligning the first course of the wall.

3 **Buttering stretcher blocks.** With the flat of a trowel, press a thick layer of mortar onto each flange of an upended stretcher block. Work the mortar until it forms a peak-shaped topping about 1 inch high. Then press the mortared flanges of the stretcher block against the flanged end of the corner block, forming a masonry joint ⅜ inch wide.

Lay the succeeding stretcher blocks, using the same buttering technique, until there is room for one last block, called the closure piece. To ensure a firm bond on the closure piece, butter the flanges at the ends of the two blocks forming the opening, as well as the flanges of the closure piece. Then insert the closure piece in the wall. On subsequent courses, stagger the location of the closure piece.

4 **Building up a lead.** Mortar the top faces of the blocks in place on the wall, then lay a second course of blocks on top of the first, staggering the position of the vertical joints. Build a stepped third and fourth course, called a lead, at each corner. Then use the leads to string a mason's line that will serve as an alignment guide for the remainder of each course.

Checking the Structure for Plumb and Level

Using a story pole. As the wall rises, check its height and the thickness of its horizontal mortar joints, using a homemade measuring tool called a story pole. To make a story pole, take a straight-edged piece of scrap lumber and use a felt-tipped pen to draw course lines at 8-inch intervals. Set the pole vertically at about 4-foot intervals along the newly laid wall to make sure a course is rising evenly. The course lines should correspond to the top of each block course.

Plumbing and leveling blocks. While the mortar joints are soft, hold a 4-foot mason's level vertically against three or more courses *(below, left)*. Nudge wayward blocks into place with the trowel handle, tapping gently to avoid breaking the masonry bonds. Then lay the level on top of a single course *(below, right)*. Use your trowel handle to make adjustments.

Checking for bulges. Use a mason's level as a straightedge, holding it horizontally along the outside face of each course *(above, left)* then diagonally along the descending corners of three or more courses *(above, right)* to check the wall for alignment. Tap with your trowel handle, as described above, to realign any mislaid blocks. Then check once again for plumb and level.

Adding Extra Strength with a Gridwork of Steel

Installing horizontal reinforcement. To reinforce horizontal joints, lay sections of steel joint-reinforcement wire into the mortared tops of every other course of bricks. Cut the wire grid to the correct lengths, using a bolt cutter or tin snips. The grid's zigzag pattern—which repeats every 16 inches, or one block length—is a handy measuring guide. Where two lengths of grid join, at corners or along a wall, overlap the two lengths of wire by the width of a block.

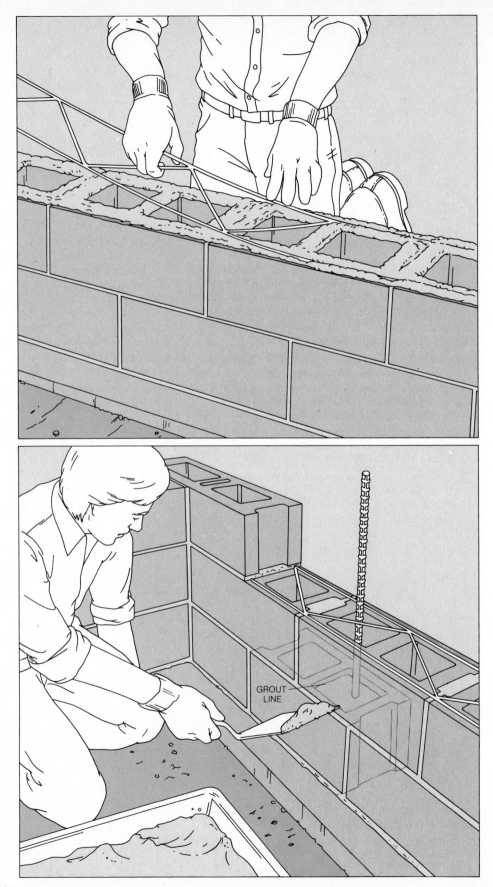

Stabilizing vertical reinforcing bar. At each point where vertical rebar rises from the footing, lower a buttered block over the rebar and set it in place. Trowel additional mortar into the cavity to anchor the rebar in the masonry wall, stopping about an inch from the top so that the anchoring mortar does not interfere with the mortar joint between courses.

Continue grouting the vertical rebar at each course, wiring additional lengths together with a 15-inch overlap to form a solid vertical reinforced column within the wall.

GROUT LINE

Tailoring Blocks to Size and Finishing the Joints

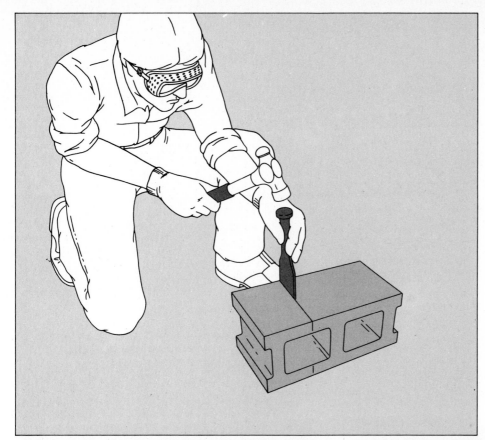

Cutting odd-sized blocks. To break a block cleanly in two, score a marked cutting line with a brickset and a ball-peen hammer. Wear goggles to protect your eyes from chips, and strike the brickset firmly but not sharply with the hammer. Move the brickset steadily across the block as you strike. Then turn the block over and score the opposite side. When the clang of the brickset against the block drops in pitch, you will know that the block has fractured. At that point, continue tapping the brickset with the hammer, but less forcefully, until the block splits evenly along the cutting line.

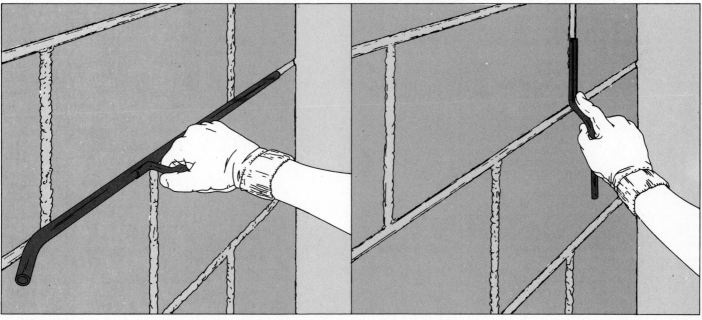

Tooling the joints. To guarantee a neat and weathertight wall, compress the mortar seams between newly laid blocks with the convex face of a jointing tool. Begin tooling when the mortar is thumbprint-hard—dry enough that it will not adhere to your skin when you press a thumb against it. Work horizontal joints first, using a 22-inch jointer (left). Then finish the vertical joints with a small 6-inch S-shaped jointing tool (right). Compact the joints with enough pressure to seal hairline cracks caused by the shrinkage of drying mortar.

After tooling the joints, trim off any remaining mortar burrs with the point of a trowel. When the joints are completely dry, after about 24 hours, groom the wall with a stiff-bristled brush to remove loose particles of mortar.

Linking Intersecting Walls with a Toothed Connection

1 **Beginning the pattern.** Wherever an interior wall joins an outer wall, substitute a 4-inch-wide partition block for the standard stretcher block in the outer wall, creating a shallow pocket. Then set another partition block, shortened by 4 inches, into the pocket, perpendicular to the outer wall. Fill in the remaining space with a partition block that has been cut 12 inches long, restoring the outer wall to its full depth.

2 **Toothing the wall.** In the second course, lay standard stretcher blocks across the outer wall. Then, on the interior wall, lay a full-sized partition block over the shortened partition block on the first course. Prop up the overhanging block with an upright 8-inch brick, mortared at both ends, or an 8-inch scrap of masonry.

Alternate these two courses as you raise the outer wall, creating a toothed joint for the interior wall while retaining the structural strength of the outer wall. After the mortar joints of the toothed blocks have set, remove the props and complete the intersecting wall.

This toothing procedure is also a practical way of creating a temporary opening in a wall, for a wheelbarrow to pass through.

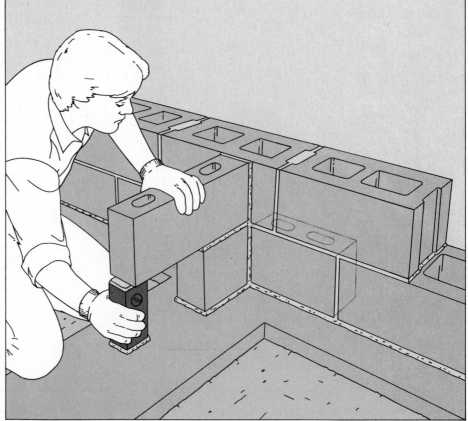

BUILDING PAPER

NEOPRENE FLANGE

FIRE CUT

TIE STRAP

Making Allowances for Floors, Doors and Windows

Setting in a control joint. Around windows and doors, where slight expansion and contraction of blocks might cause cracks to appear in the wall, create vertical control joints. Place each joint at the edge of one side of the frame, using a combination of full and half blocks, in order to produce a continuous line. Before mortaring the joint on each course, press a square of building paper against the end of one block; this prevents the mortar from bonding to that surface. Allow enough slack in the paper for it to follow the contours of the block end. Lay the adjoining block in the usual fashion. The building paper eliminates the bond and allows some slippage in the joint, so that the wall will respond to stress without cracking.

After completing the joint, rake out a groove ¾ inch deep down its full length, and pack the groove with flexible caulking compound to seal the joint against weather. An alternate seal, available from many block manufacturers, is a neoprene flange that slips into a precast slot in a special control block (inset). The flange works as a control joint and also acts as a seal, making caulking unnecessary.

Securing floor joists. In every course where joists intersect an outer wall, substitute partition blocks for standard stretcher blocks along the affected wall, creating a 4-inch-deep ledge. At every joist position, install two joist anchors, one on each side of the joist. Cut and shape each anchor from a 12-inch length of perforated sheet-metal tie strap; bury one end of the anchor in the mortar-filled cavity of the underlying block, leaving about 6 inches free. Position the joist on the ledge, and nail the free ends of the anchors to the side of the joist. Fill the spaces between joists with partition blocks cut 13½ inches long, leaving a ½-inch space on both sides of the joist to keep moisture from collecting.

Before installing each joist, cut both ends at an angle, so that the joist top is 4 inches shorter overall than the bottom. This angle, called a fire cut, allows a burning joist to fall free of its masonry pocket without rupturing the wall.

Installing door and window frames. When the block wall reaches door or window height, frame the opening with pressure-treated 2-by-8 lumber. Erect the vertical framing first, then add the horizontal. For a door, cut the vertical framing to fit between floor level and a point 1¾ inches short of the top of the opening; for a window, cut it 3½ inches shorter than the overall height of the opening. Mortar pieces of scrap lumber into the concave ends of the concrete blocks (*inset*); these scraps will serve as nailing anchors for the framing. To assemble the frame, set the vertical members in place and brace them with lengths of scrap lumber while you nail them to the wall. Then attach the top frame to the vertical members. For a window, add a bottom frame, nailing it to blocks mortared into the tops of the course of blocks below. After the wall is complete, caulk the joint where the wood and the masonry come together.

Metal doorframes and window frames come equipped with projecting anchors; these are simply mortared into place to secure the frame.

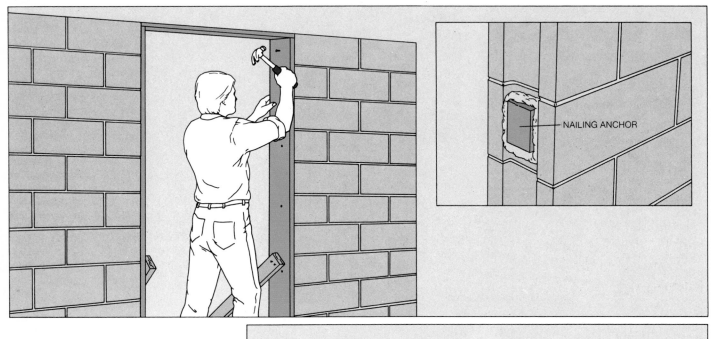

NAILING ANCHOR

HOIST STANDARD

Raising a lintel. To set a precast concrete lintel over a door or window opening, hoist it into place with a heavy-duty rope-and-pulley system rigged to a rotating hoist standard, an upright support that swivels in a socket provided for it on most scaffolding systems. Position two helpers on the scaffolding's walk board to receive the lintel and maneuver it into place on the wall. Then make a sling by running two lengths of rope through holes near the ends of a scrap 2-by-4. Make sure the 2-by-4 is balanced in the loops and the block is balanced in the sling before raising it off the ground. Mortar the ends of the lintel, and swing it into position on the wall.

ANCHOR BOLT

Built-in Hardware and an Extra Band of Steel

Anchoring the sill plate. To set anchor bolts for a sill plate—the heavy board that underpins a wood-frame structure—mark positions for the bolts along the top of the concrete-block wall. There should be bolts at the corners, on both sides of a door, and at 4-foot intervals in between. Cut a jig for each bolt from scraps of 2-by-8, and drill a center hole in each ⅛ inch larger than the diameter of the bolt. Slip the bolt through the jig and secure it with a washer and nut.

At every bolt location, fill the core of the block with mortar and set the jig over the block. When the mortar has hardened, remove the nuts and washers and pull away the jigs. Unroll strips of sill-sealing paper across the top of the wall, pushing the paper down over the protruding boltheads. Then with the paper pattern, drill matching holes in the sole plate and fasten it to the boltheads, using thin wooden shims between the wall top and the sill plate to level it before tightening the nuts.

Assembling a bond-beam cap. To reinforce the top of a high block wall, lay a top course of specially channeled speed blocks, inset with two rows of steel rebar. At each corner use ordinary corner blocks, notching their partition walls with a brickset to make the channeling continuous. Set ½-inch rebar into the channel in parallel rows 2 inches apart. Overlap lengths of bar 15 inches and wire them together. At corners, bend the bar into a 90° angle, as described on page 43. When the rebar is in place, fill the channel with mortar and embed in it anchor bolts for roof framing, as for a sill plate (*above*).

Covering a Frame House with a Brick Veneer

If you could poke hard enough at a brick house built in the last 25 years, you would probably find that the brickwork was only skin deep. The house would actually have an outer wall, one brick thick, separated by an air space from an inner wood-frame wall. Such a combination wall, called brick veneer, is far less costly than a solid brick wall but yields many of solid brick's advantages: It is more resistant to weather than plain wood siding; it protects the house from external fires; and it requires very little maintenance. In addition, the air space between the two walls provides a measure of insulation.

Most brick veneer is applied as a finishing touch; the techniques used to sheathe a new house with brick can be adapted to covering the worn or damaged siding of an older house—if the building meets certain conditions. The foundation footing must be wide enough to accommodate the extra layer of brickwork or, for a deep foundation, the extra layer of 4-inch concrete block on which the new brickwork will rest. On most houses, the footing extends 4 inches beyond the foundation, ample for a new wall. You will also have to check whether the overhang of the eaves will accommodate the thicker wall and, if not, whether it is possible to extend them.

Once you have determined that the veneering is feasible, you will have to submit a plan for your project to the local building department for approval. If the veneer will be supported by a second foundation wall, the plan should include details for this feature. The supporting wall will be built in the same way as the concrete-block foundation wall that is described on page 74.

Before the bricklaying can begin, you will need to cover the existing siding with roofing felt, extend the window and door casings with moldings deep enough to meet the new brickwork, and locate wall studs to serve as a point of attachment for the corrugated-steel ties that will anchor the brickwork to the existing walls. To probe for these studs, use an electric drill fitted with a slender bit.

The final step in the preliminaries is mathematical: Plot the placement of the courses, which may have to be adjusted vertically in order to avoid splitting bricks horizontally as you build around windows, over doors or under the soffit at the eaves. If you plan to enliven the brickwork with quoins, decorative patterns or arches *(page 98, page 112)*, plot a section of the wall on graph paper.

To estimate the number of bricks you will need for a single-thickness wall, measure the area to be veneered in square feet and multiply that figure by 6.75—the number of standard bricks, plus their mortar joints, that fill one square foot. Add 5 per cent to that amount to allow for breakage and mistakes in cutting. Figure on 10 cubic feet of mortar for every 100 square feet of bricks, the mortar to be made of mortar cement mixed with sand and water. A 70-pound bag of mortar cement mixed with sand in a 1-to-3 ratio by volume will yield about 3 cubic feet of mortar.

To tie the bricks to the wall, you will need 22-gauge corrugated-steel wall ties, ⅞ inch wide and 7 inches long. Normally, one of these will be set for every 12 bricks, but on gables the ties fall more frequently: one for every six bricks. You will also need L-shaped 3½-by-3½-inch steel lintels, ¼ inch thick, to carry the brickwork across the tops of windows and doors, and 6-mil polyethylene flashing to seal veneer walls at ground level and around windows and doors. The lintels are available from masonry suppliers in lengths as short as 24 inches. Flashing is available from building suppliers.

Finally, rent enough scaffolding to raise you, a helper, and a load of bricks and mortar to the height of the eaves. And do your bricklaying in good weather, when neither rain nor freezing temperatures will adversely affect the mortar.

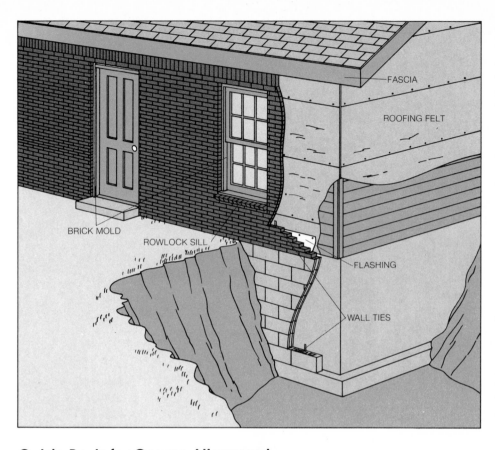

FASCIA

ROOFING FELT

BRICK MOLD

ROWLOCK SILL

FLASHING

WALL TIES

Anatomy of a veneered wood-frame wall. The brick facing applied to a wood-frame house rests on a 4-inch concrete-block foundation, built on the outer ledge of the house footing but separated from the foundation by a ½-inch air space. At every two courses of block, corrugated-steel wall ties are anchored in the mortar joints and nailed to the existing foundation with masonry nails, using a power stud driver (*page 20*).

The veneer bricks stand 1 inch out from the siding; wall ties anchor them every six courses to the wall studs. Overlapping sheets of 15-pound roofing felt, held with roofing nails, protect the siding from moisture in the air space. Flashing and strategically placed weep holes (*page 94*)—at the bottom of the veneer wall, above windows and doors, and below sills—direct the moisture out of the cavity.

Wood molding 1 inch thick and 2¼ inches wide, called brick mold, is added to extend the original window casings and door frames. Hidden under the bricks, heavy steel lintels provide support over the windows and doors. Below each existing sill, rowlocks—bricks set on edge—create a second sill, angled to shed water. The veneer wall rises to within ¼ inch of the soffit—the underside of the roof overhang—where a frieze board or a molding strip hides the gap.

Guide Posts for Course Alignment

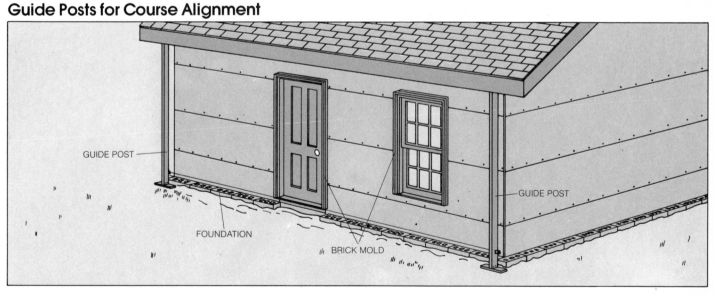

GUIDE POST

GUIDE POST

FOUNDATION

BRICK MOLD

A system for marking course levels. To simplify adjustments in course placement when raising bricks against an existing wall, erect two straight 2-by-4 guide posts, one at each end of the wall. Position the posts so that the distance between their inner faces and the wall is equal to the thickness of a brick, plus an allowance of 1 inch for the air space between the wall and the brick veneer. Plumb the 2-by-4s, and toenail them into the soffit at the eaves and into wood base plates at ground level.

Mark each post with the spacing between courses, calculated to make splitting bricks unnecessary as you build from the foundation to the soffit. First, measure and rule off a whole number of courses between the foundation and the bottom of the rowlock sills, which will extend 4½ inches below the existing windowsills. Then measure and rule off the courses between the bottom of the rowlock sills and the top of the wood brick mold that frames the tops of the windows and doors. Finally, measure and

mark off the courses between the brick mold and the soffit.

Within each calibrated band, you can vary the width of mortar joints from as little as ¼ inch to as much as ½ inch in order to divide the band into whole-brick courses. If windows are at different heights, you must choose one sill as the reference level and cut bricks to fit the others; the reference level should be the one at which split bricks would be most conspicuous.

Raising the Veneer to Lintel Height

1 **Laying the first course.** Lay a dry row of bricks along the top of the block foundation, extending the first brick 5 inches beyond the corner of the house. Adjust the width of the mortar joints so that the last brick extends 1 inch or 5 inches beyond the far corner. Set aside the bricks spanning the door opening, and cut the bricks abutting the door so that they will fit flush with the brick mold framing the door. Stretch a mason's line between the first-course markings on the guideposts, and mortar the bricks in place, outer faces flush with the mason's line. To mortar the bricks, set them aside three or four at a time, spread a bed of mortar on the foundation, then butter the ends of the bricks and position them in the mortar.

At each corner, lay a perpendicular brick *(inset)* 1 inch out from the adjacent wall. As the courses rise, these perpendicular corner bricks will create a toothed edge to serve as a guide for the mason's line on the adjacent wall. As you build up the wall, you can mortar half bricks beneath projecting corner bricks to provide temporary support; each half brick is removed as the next course fixes the corner brick in place.

2 **Flashing the brickwork.** Add another course, if necessary, to bring the top of the veneer just above ground level. As you work, use your trowel to scoop up excess mortar squeezed into the air space behind the veneer. Spread a strip of 6-mil polyethylene flashing, 12 inches wide, along the top course of bricks, extending it over the air space and up the backup wall. Adjust the strip so that the lower edge lies 1 inch in from the face of the brickwork, and fasten the other edge to the backup wall with closely spaced roofing nails. Spread a bed of mortar over the plastic and lay the next course of bricks.

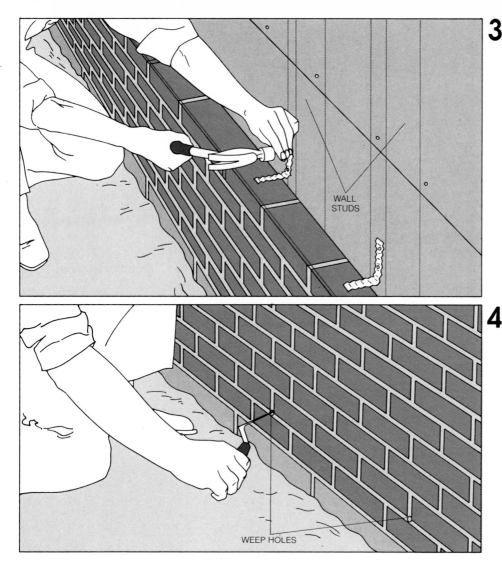

3 **Anchoring the veneer.** When the veneer is six courses high, secure it to the backup wall with corrugated wall ties. Crease each tie at its midpoint to form a right angle, rest one leg on the brickwork and nail the other leg of the angle to a wall stud, using eightpenny (2½-inch) nails. Then spread mortar and lay the next course of bricks to embed the ties firmly in the masonry.

WALL STUDS

4 **Opening a way for trapped moisture.** About an hour after laying the flashing, when the mortar in the first few courses has stiffened a little, finish the mortar joints in the bottom two or three courses with a jointing tool. Then, using a tuck pointer—a slender tool generally used as a joint filler—bore weep holes through the mortar at the bottom of every third vertical joint in the course directly above the flashing, taking care not to puncture the flashing. Rotate the tuck pointer to widen the hole.

Continue to raise the veneer wall, adding wall ties every six courses, until you are 4½ inches below a window sill. Leaving a 4½-inch gap beneath the sill, raise the wall to the top of the window; cut bricks as necessary to butt against the vertical brick mold nailed to the window casing.

WEEP HOLES

Carrying the Brickwork over Windows and Doors

1 **Positioning the lintel.** Move the mason's line out of your way, and lay a length of steel lintel across the top of each door or window opening, extending it at least 8 inches on either side. Align the vertical flange of the lintel so that its forward face is flush with the back face of the bricks on which it rests. Fill in the ½-inch space between the front face of the bricks and the front edge of the lintel with a band of mortar, scraped from the back of the trowel.

LINTEL VERTICAL FLANGE

2 **Setting bricks over the lintel.** Cut a strip of 12-inch-wide flashing the length of the lintel. Lay the flashing against the lintel, positioning the lower edge of the flashing ½ inch in from the forward edge of the lintel. Carry the flashing up the back of the lintel and across the air space between the house wall and the veneer; nail the flashing to the house wall. Adjust the mason's line and lay the next course. Over the lintel, join the bricks end to end with mortar, but omit the bed of mortar beneath them.

Continue to build up the veneer wall with succeeding courses. Then, about an hour after the lintel bricks have been laid, finish the mortar joints and pierce every third vertical joint above the lintel with a weep hole.

A Frieze of Soldier Bricks to Cap the Wall

Topping the brickwork. When the veneer wall is three courses below the soffit, lay a final course of soldiers—bricks set on end. Set up the mason's line on the guide posts, positioning it ¼ inch below the soffit, and spread a mortar bed over the last course of horizontal bricks. Then butter one bed side of each soldier brick and stand it on the mortar bed, lining up the top of the brick with the mason's line. Tilt the bricks as necessary to slide them into position in the space remaining between the wall and the soffit. When you are about six bricks from the end of this course, set the last bricks dry, to adjust the mortar joints so that the soldier course will end even with the corner. Use a crayon to mark the positions of the bricks on the course below. Then remove the dry bricks and mortar them back in place.

To complete a veneer wall under a gable, raise the wall to the eave level, then erect three-course leads (page 76) at both ends of the topmost course (inset). Cut the outer bricks at an angle to fit snugly under the sloping soffit. String a mason's line between the leads, and lay the intermediate bricks. To anchor the mason's line, drive nails into the mortar joints. Tie the veneer to the house wall with brick ties every third course. Repeat until the veneer wall is completed. Cover the ragged edge of the sloping brickwork with a strip of moulding or an overhanging frieze board.

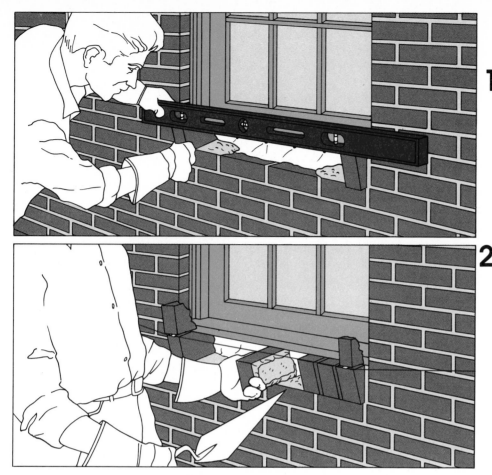

Finishing the Window with a Rowlock Sill

1 **Setting the end bricks.** Seal the 4½-inch opening below each window with a 12-inch-wide strip of flashing. Spread the flashing across the bricks and over the air space; nail it to the backup wall *(page 86)*. Cut two bricks to 5 inches in length and mortar them in place at the ends of the opening, angling the bricks slightly downward. Check that both bricks protrude equally from the wall face—usually ½ inch—and hold a level across the top of the bricks to be sure they lie at the same angle.

2 **Adding intermediate bricks.** Set in 5-inch bricks dry to space the joints. Using crayon, mark their positions on the window sill.

Adjust the mason's line *(page 85)* until it runs level with the tops of the end bricks. To hold it flush with the outer edges of the end bricks, bend scraps of cardboard around the line and clamp down both line and cardboard under scrap bricks. Butter and lay the sill bricks, aligning them with the marks and the line.

After an hour or so, finish all of the mortar joints except the horizontal joint beneath the rowlock sill. Pierce this joint with three or four evenly spaced weep holes *(page 87)*.

Brick Veneering over Concrete Block

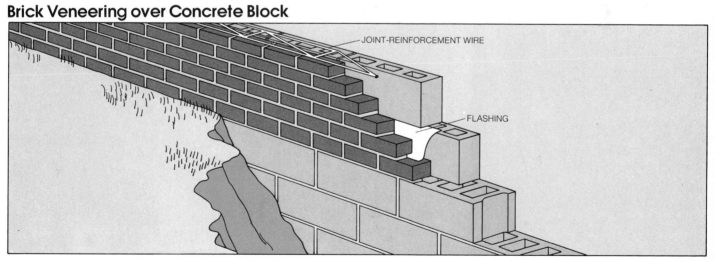

JOINT-REINFORCEMENT WIRE

FLASHING

Anatomy of a brick-faced masonry wall. When brick veneer is backed up by a concrete-block wall—often called a masonry-cavity wall—bricks and blocks rise together, with a 1-inch air space between them. Both the 4-inch concrete-block backup wall *(page 85)* and the brick veneer share an 8-inch concrete-block foundation wall *(page 74)*. The two layers are tied together every six brick courses with joint-reinforcement wire, straddling both layers.

Because in this case no existing wall is present to support guide posts for the courses of masonry, stepped-back corner leads have to be erected for both the brick wall and the concrete-block wall. Steel joint-reinforcement wire is installed in the leads at the appropriate course levels. Each piece of wire is cut 12 inches longer than the length of the lead itself so that it will overlap the joint reinforcement in the intermediate bricks or blocks, to be laid later.

Flashing seals the cavity between the two walls—just as for brick veneer over wood siding. It is placed in the same locations, anchored to mortar joints in the backup wall. Flashing is also installed in the appropriate courses of the corner leads. It should be cut 4 inches longer than the lead, to overlap the flashing on later bricks. Brick rowlock sills and the brickwork above lintels are constructed just as they are on a brick-veneer wall erected over wood framing.

The Age-Old Art of Building a Stone Wall

Stone masonry is based on the principle that no two stones have exactly the same shape. Unlike factory-made bricks and blocks, which fit together in neat rectangular patterns, irregularly shaped stones form a random mosaic that can never be duplicated. The unique shapes of stones account for much of stonework's beauty but they also pose its greatest problem: When stones are being laid, every one needs a firm support on which to rest.

The bottom course in any stone wall—whether freestanding (below) or veneer (opposite, top)—must be supported by a sturdy frost-proof footing (page 40). The stones lying on the footing must be bedded solidly in the mortar to prevent them from shifting or slipping on the flat surface of the concrete slab.

Because the stones' weight would force mortar of normal consistency out of the joints, use a stiffer mixture for stone masonry than for bricks or blocks. Combine three parts portland cement to one part sand, but add only enough water—usually about 20 per cent less than normal (page 74)—to make a mixture that can be squeezed into a compact ball.

When you are ready to begin work, sort through your stones and save the obvious corner pieces—the ones with two flat faces that meet in a neat 90° angle or that can be easily squared by cutting (page 12). Also make a mental note of the proportion of roughly rectangular stones to those without any particular shape, and the proportion of large stones to small ones. As you lay up the wall, use stones in the same proportions, regularly incorporating different sizes and shapes for a balanced appearance.

When laying stone, proceed slowly and deliberately, respecting each piece for the esthetic and structural opportunities it presents. Trowel a firm, flat bed of mortar for each stone to rest on. Position stones on the wall so that their top surfaces are level or slope down toward the core. The mortar joints may weaken over time, but the pull of gravity will help keep the stones in place.

Keep the first course of stones in alignment by sighting along building lines strung from batter boards (page 28). Then switch to a mason's line stretched between nails or line pins pegged in the mortar joints. As you work, always try to place a large, heavy stone over two or three smaller ones to spread and balance its weight. And, to prevent vertical rifts in the wall, avoid aligning vertical joints from course to course.

And be patient: An experienced mason can lay 400 square feet of concrete block a day, but a master stone mason averages only 50 square feet of stonework.

Two Ways to Use Stone: Solid and Veneered

A double-thick stone wall. A stone garden wall consisting of two faces of large and small rocks sits squarely upon a wide, sturdy poured-concrete footing. Joining the footing and the first course—which consists of large blocks that fit together easily—is a thick, level bed of mortar. Stones in the remaining courses are mixed, large and small. Irregular stones—called chinking stones—fill large gaps between stones. Stone chips and mortar fill the core between the two faces of the wall. Traversing the core every 2 to 3 feet are long tie stones, which, like header bricks (page 99), bond together the two wall faces. For extra strength, vertical mortar joints are staggered from course to course. A 2½-inch-thick flagstone coping, mortared in place, provides a weatherproof cap.

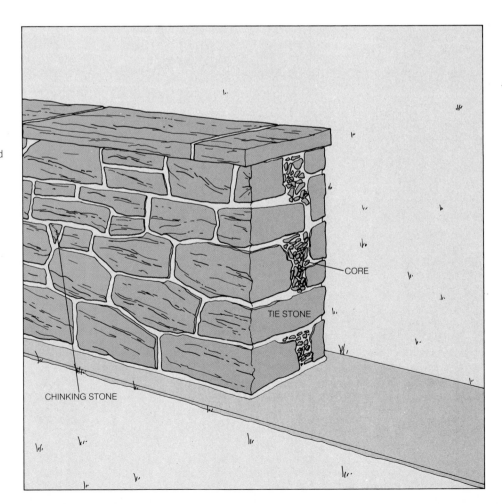

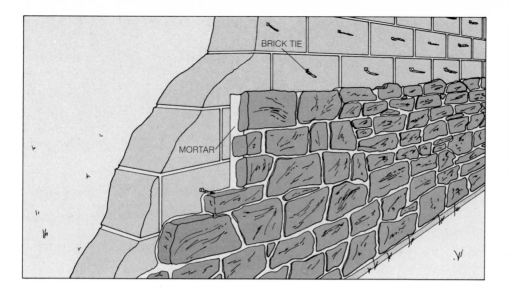

A stone-veneer wall. A single thickness of stone, self-supporting but essentially decorative, rests on the same footing as the concrete-block wall that it covers. The pattern of the stones reflects the masonry principles used to erect freestanding walls—although a veneer wall does not support a structure, it must support itself. Stones are set firmly in position, with mortar at their backs as well as above and below. Strengthening the mortar bond between the block wall and the stone veneer are bendable sheet-metal brick ties *(page 87)* nailed into each block.

Mortaring the First Course

1 **Setting the cornerstones.** Spread a mortar bed 1 inch thick atop the footing, aligning it with strings previously stretched between the building lines marked on the batter boards. Lay the cornerstone on the mortar, aligning it too with the building lines. With a tuck pointer, force more mortar between the footing and the stone until the two corner faces of the stone are plumb. Go on with the first course, using large rocks that fit together easily; leave a ¾-inch gap between stones. At every corner, use a cornerstone.

If, after setting a stone, you decide to move it, lift it out and wash it thoroughly to remove unwanted mortar. When the first course is completed, take away the building-line strings.

2 **Filling vertical joints.** Scoop up mortar on a trowel and, using the trowel as a palette, pack mortar into the vertical gaps between stones with a tuck pointer. Fill the joints until the stones are firmly wedged together; do not push in too much mortar, or you will force the stones out of position. If mortar begins to ooze out of a joint, catch it with the point of the trowel and dump it into the core of the wall.

3 **Building up the core.** After laying the first course, drop small stones and shards into the core between the two thicknesses, and bond the chips and scraps together with additional mortar, thinned to a consistency that makes it easy to work around the stones. When the core is filled level with the top of the first course, trowel on a new mortar bed, but do not smooth it; leave it loose enough to conform to the bottom surfaces of the next course of stones. Lay cornerstones at both ends of the next course, then at the corners of the wall insert nails or line pins in the mortar joints and string a mason's line *(page 88)*. The line will help you keep the face of the wall plumb as you work.

After laying each course, fill and level the core. Then lay cornerstones for the next course and move the mason's line up to the next level. Cap the wall with 2½-inch slabs of flagstone; these will keep it weathertight.

Balancing Stones With Irregular Shapes

Chinking large gaps. If a large gap occurs between two stones, use a mason's hammer to tap a small stone—a chinking stone—into the unsightly joint. Choose a chinking stone that not only improves the wall's appearance but helps level the top of the course to receive the stone above.

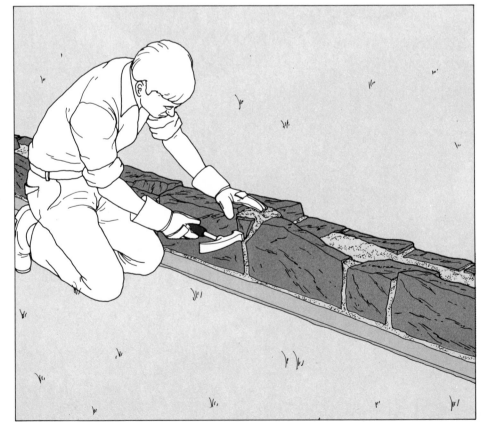

Shimming and shoring stones. If the irregular bottom of a stone makes it wobble, wedge a V-shaped stone chip—called a shim—into the mortar underneath *(below, left)*. Leave the shim in place to steady the stone and keep it aligned until the mortar sets. Then chisel out the shim and fill the hole with fresh mortar.

For a teetering stone that is too large to be steadied with a stone shim, use a 2-by-4 board as a diagonal brace instead. Position the length of 2-by-4 at the correct angle to support the stone, then anchor the board at ground level with a heavy rock *(below, right)*. When the mortar has set, remove the wooden brace.

Dressing mortar joints. After the mortar in each joint has been allowed to set for 30 to 45 minutes, offset the stones by using a pointing trowel to strike, or finish, the joints. Adjust the depth of the joint to the size and shape of the stones that surround it. Then use a stiff-bristled brush, such as an old paintbrush or a whisk broom, to smooth the remaining mortar.

A Block Wall to Retain a Soil Embankment

Holding back a mass of earth—whether to control erosion on a hillside, shore up the excavation beside a widened driveway or finish the sidewalk edge of a sloping lawn—calls for the sturdy barrier of a retaining wall. Retaining walls can be formed and poured just like the large-scale concrete walls shown on pages 52-61, but concrete block offers an economical and easy alternative. Although a concrete-block retaining wall is built by the same techniques as an ordinary freestanding concrete-block wall (*pages 74-79*), the stresses placed on it demand a very different design.

Most walls are buffeted only by wind, but a retaining wall must withstand soil pressures of hundreds of pounds per square foot. This is multiplied many times over after rain, when water adds weight to the soil. And the pressure is increased still further when a heavy object, such as a car, rests on the surface of the backed-up soil (in the argot of structural engineers, the additional stress is called a surcharge).

In order to provide the requisite strength, a retaining wall must be reinforced, and the nature of the reinforcement varies with the stresses to which the wall will be subjected. Assessing these stresses and allowing for them demands expert knowledge. It is essential that you secure the services of a structural engineer for any retaining wall higher than 4 feet. Even for a lower wall, the advice of a professional engineer is desirable, although a building inspector intimately acquainted with local soil conditions and construction practices can often help you plan a retaining wall.

Into the engineering calculations must go figures for the height of the soil to be retained—measured in feet above ground level—and for the steepness of its slope. Another factor, estimated by means of test borings, is the bearing pressure of the soil on which the wall will stand—that is, the ability of the soil to support a load. The combined weight of

the wall itself and the backfill must never exceed the soil's bearing pressure.

Armed with this information, the engineer will write plans and specifications for a footing and wall strong enough to stand up to the job. Chances are that the plan will call for a wall resembling one of the four common types illustrated opposite and on the following pages. Three are heavily reinforced—vertically with steel rods and horizontally with strips of joint-reinforcement wire. They are designed to resist extreme stresses, and they contain more steel than the average wall is likely to need. The fourth type, called a gravity wall, contains no steel; it is a time-honored design that relies for strength on its great mass of masonry. Because gravity walls require far more labor than those reinforced with steel, engineers seldom specify them for any structure more than 3 or 4 feet high.

Today the most commonly used design for retaining walls is the cantilever, so named because the wall is structurally tied to one end of a footing that extends far back into the earth; thus the same great mass of earth pressing against the back of the wall is also pressing downward against the cantilevered footing, in effect holding the two in balance.

If conditions demand that your wall needs more bracing than a cantilever provides, it can be further strengthened with concrete-block abutments placed either behind or in front of the wall and secured to the footing with vertical rebar. When tied to the back of the wall, the abutments are called counterforts; they resist the pressure of the soil by pulling the wall backward, into the earth. The counterforts are strengthened with steel joint reinforcement and are eventually hidden under backfill. When placed at the front of the wall, the abutments are called buttresses and remain exposed. They resist the pressure of the soil by pushing against it—and because concrete is at its strongest when under pressure, they require no additional steel.

Counterfort walls and buttressed walls are generally considered equally strong; the choice of one over the other will depend largely on appearance and space. A counterfort wall is less intrusive; it looks like any other wall. A buttressed wall, with its exposed supports, is a powerful visual element in the landscape, but its need for room can be a drawback: Buttresses could carry the retaining wall too close to the property line or could encroach on a garden at the wall's base.

Drainage is another consideration in the design of a retaining wall. In most cases water is allowed to escape from the soil behind the wall either through weep holes—small openings in the wall—or by means of a sloping arrangement of perforated pipe that carries the water down to the ends of the wall.

Careful construction is, of course, imperative. Be sure to mix the concrete for the footing properly and pour it so that the base of the footing lies below the frost line (*page 40*). Lay up the block perfectly plumb, and form any corners carefully. Place steel reinforcement in both the footing and the wall (*page 74*) in the precise locations specified by the plan. Finally parge, or coat, the back of the wall with waterproofing compound to divert all seepage to the weep holes or drainpipes (*page 97*).

To ensure that the mortar in a retaining wall cures sufficiently, wait at least 10 days before backfilling the area behind the wall with soil. Usually the backfill can be the soil removed during the wall's construction, but in some cases the engineer may specify a special free-draining backfill, such as gravel or granular soil, which must be ordered from a building-supply dealer. You will also need coarse gravel or stone to back up the line of weep holes or cradle the drainage pipe, to prevent them from becoming clogged with dirt. Count on about 2 cubic feet of gravel or stone per foot of wall for the weep holes, and about 1 cubic foot for every foot of pipe.

Four Common Types of Retaining Wall

A cantilever wall. Placed near the front of a reinforced footing, a cantilever wall is secured to it with bent sections of rebar; one end of each rod lies horizontally within the footing, the other rises vertically through the bottom two courses of concrete block. There are additional lengths of vertical rebar, lowered through the hollow blocks, that lock together the courses; strips of joint reinforcement, buried in each horizontal mortar joint, reinforce the link between blocks in each course. In order to bind the rebar and blocks together, the cores of any blocks through which the rebar passes are filled with grout, a soupy mortar mixture. On the top, the wall is capped with solid blocks to prevent water from entering the unfilled block cores; near the bottom there is a row of weep holes to allow water to drain from behind the wall.

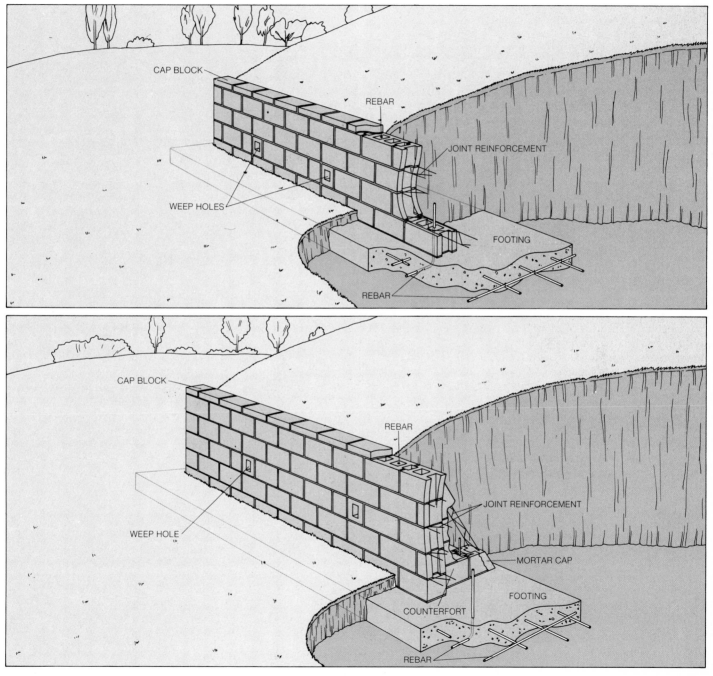

A counterfort wall. Similar to the cantilever wall (*above*), this wall is braced by triangular concrete-block counterforts at intervals along the back. The counterforts are tied to the footing with bent rebar and to the wall with horizontal strips of joint reinforcement, as intersecting bearing walls are joined together (*page 76*). A strip of joint reinforcement also strengthens the counterfort; its sloping surface is formed by shearing off the top corners of the concrete blocks and capping them with mortar to shed water. The cores of these sheared blocks are covered with metal mesh to keep mortar from falling through. When completed, the counterforts are buried under backfill.

A buttressed wall. Braced by concrete-block buttresses across its face, this wall is set close to the rear of the footing. The forward edge of the footing is notched between the buttresses to reduce the weight of the wall. The wall's interior reinforcement is just like that of a cantilever wall *(page 95),* and its buttresses are tied to it the same way counterforts are connected to a wall. Both the wall and its stepped buttresses are capped with solid concrete blocks; behind the wall a sloping, perforated drainpipe, embedded in gravel, carries away water.

A gravity wall. This type of wall is a succession of concrete-block faces that descend, from front to back, in pyramid fashion, each face one course shorter than the one before. Mortar alone joins the structure to its footing and its faces to each other. The hollow top blocks of each face are capped with solid blocks to seal out water. A slanting drainpipe, embedded in gravel, carries away water that collects behind the wall. When completed, the back assembly is buried with backfill, so that only the sheer face of the wall is exposed.

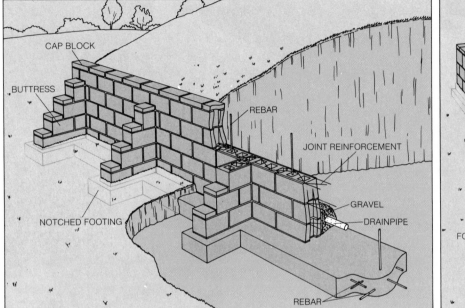

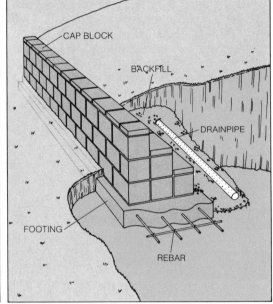

Measures to Prevent Water from Weakening the Wall

Capping the top. After laying the last course of hollow blocks, lay one solid block, 4 inches thick, atop each end of the wall. Measure the distance between these two solid blocks, and mark the center point between them with chalk. Stretch a mason's line between the two cap blocks *(page 75, Step 3)* and, using the line as a guide, lay solid blocks from one end of the wall toward the center point. Stop when the last block hits the center point or falls half a block length short of it—it must do one or the other because the blocks are modular. Lay blocks from the other end of the wall to finish the cap.

Setting weep holes. At every point where the plan calls for a weep hole, lay a square, single-core block on its side so that the core opens through the wall. Next to this one, lay a second square block, core up; it will reestablish the running-bond pattern of the wall. After you have completed this course, lay another full course on top of it. Then trowel mortar around the back edges of the single-core blocks and embed a square of coarse galvanized screening or hardware cloth in the mortar. This will keep debris out of the weep holes.

When backfilling, use soil until you reach the top of the course just below the weep holes. Then spread gravel behind the entire course containing the weep holes; extend the layer of gravel to the back edge of the excavation (*inset*). Finish backfilling with soil above the gravel.

Installing drainpipes. Backfill behind the wall to a depth of about 12 inches above the footing, mounding the soil about 6 inches higher at the center of the wall. Cover the soil with three inches of gravel or crushed stone. Cut two lengths of 3-inch perforated pipe long enough to reach from the top of the mound to 6 inches beyond the end of the wall. Place a square of fine galvanized screening over the high end of each pipe (*page 63*) to keep the pipe free of soil and small stones. Cover the pipes with 3 inches of gravel or stone. Finish backfilling with soil.

Setting Bricks in Decorative Patterns

A brick wall is above all else functional. But with variations of the conventional elements of bricklaying, a wall that defines a property line or encloses a garden can also be decorative. In its simplest form, this secondary role rings changes on the traditional bonds, or patterns, in which bricks are laid. Or it combines differently colored bricks. But bricks can also be offset from the wall plane to create contrapuntal effects of light and shadow or to accent a corner with an architectural device called a quoin.

One decorative variant of brickwork is to make a lattice, screening an area while allowing breezes to pass through. Another is to break up the masonry mass with graceful serpentine curves. In addition, specially cast coping bricks can be used to finish a wall with an ornamental cap, and mortar joints can be tinted to vary their color or specially tooled to vary their shape.

Most brick walls are built two bricks thick and are bound together at intervals by bricks set crosswise, across both thicknesses. In modern practice these crosswise bricks are often replaced by metal strips or wires embedded crosswise in the mortar joints of both wall thicknesses. Such walls adapt easily to any decorative treatment based on colored bricks, on variations in the arrangement of lengthwise and crosswise bricks (commonly called stretchers and headers) or on reliefs created by offsetting bricks. But even the single thickness of a brick-veneer wall responds to patterned brickwork created in this fashion: Header bricks are simply replaced by half bricks.

Lattice and serpentine walls, however, are laid in a single thickness, and the consequent loss in strength sets limits on the way they can be used. An openwork or curved brick wall generally should not be more than 4 feet tall. And although a serpentine wall in effect braces itself, a lattice wall needs to be buttressed every 6 to 10 feet with brick piers 12 to 16 inches square.

Like any brick wall, a decorative one requires a poured-concrete footing (page 40). For walls more than 4 feet high, the rules for foundation depth and size are threefold: The slab must rest on soil below the frost line—often several feet down; its vertical thickness must equal the thickness of the wall it supports, and it must be at least twice as wide as it is thick. A brick wall less than 4 feet high, however, can rest on a slab buried just below grade level, providing the surrounding soil supplies good drainage. To aid drainage, a bed of gravel should be laid beneath the footing. Such a slab should be about 8 inches thick and 4 inches wider than the thickness of the wall it supports.

To be sure the structure you plan is suitable for your soil conditions and conforms to the local building codes, check with your local building department. If the wall will rise near a property line, discuss your plans with your neighbor.

A decorative wall, especially one that involves a complex pattern or bricks of varying colors, needs a preliminary sketch of one complete unit of the design. This not only is essential for ordering the bricks but is also helpful later on, in setting the bricks. Use graph paper for the sketch, drawing in the individual bricks but increasing their size by ⅜ inch in every dimension to allow for the mortar joints. Indicate any shifts in color with a colored pencil.

Bricks come in a virtually endless variety of colors, sizes and textures; consider the options listed on pages 8-9 before making your sketch. Then, before you order the bricks, use the formula on page 84 to determine the number of bricks and the amount of mortar the wall will require. Be sure to buy 5 per cent more bricks than the calculated amount to cover breakage.

In choosing your bricks, keep in mind that cored bricks, though they are easier to break and are suitable for most patterned walls, cannot be used for latticework or for offset bricks. Solid bricks are also essential for capping walls and piers. Remember, too, that most bricks are made to be exposed on one side only, and that the opposite face is often unattractive. For single-thickness walls, choose bricks with two finished faces.

In the actual building of the wall, decorative brickwork calls for a few variations in standard bricklaying techniques. Offset bricks should be laid in smooth mortar beds rather than the furrowed mortar of conventional bricklaying. Unlike ordinary joints, these joints should not be tooled into a concave shape. Instead, simply trim them flush, using a long slender mortar tool called a tuck pointer. For latticework, many of the mortar joints will consist of no more than a pat of mortar. In this case, the mortar bed will require neither furrowing nor smoothing.

Like all straight walls, straight decorative walls should be erected between a pair of stepped brick leads, carefully plumbed and leveled and checked for vertical spacing with a story pole (page 76). A mason's line, strung between the leads, ensures horizontal alignment of the intermediate bricks. With single-thickness walls and lattice walls, careful checks for horizontal and vertical alignment are especially important, since any misalignment can seriously weaken a thin brick wall.

Enlivening a Brick Wall with Geometric Designs

Simple decorative bonds. These three patterns alternate stretcher bricks, used lengthwise, with header bricks, set crosswise. Originally designed to strengthen double-thickness walls by binding the two layers together *(inset)*, they can be adapted to brick-veneer walls *(page 84)* and single-thickness walls if half bricks are substituted for the wall-through headers.

Common bond *(top)* interrupts conventional rows of stretchers with a row of headers or half bricks at every fifth, sixth or seventh course. English bond *(center)* alternates courses of headers and stretchers. In Flemish bond *(bottom)* the headers and stretchers are alternated in each course. With all of these bonds, use whole bricks, half bricks, or three-quarter bricks, as needed, to bring the courses even at the ends of walls.

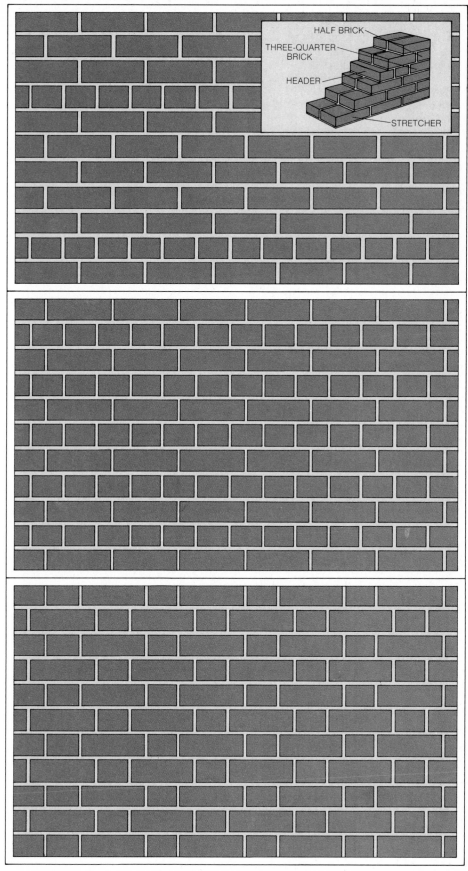

Three variants on Flemish bond. More elaborate ornamental bonds, such as the three geometric patterns illustrated here, incorporate Flemish courses, consisting of both headers and stretchers, and employ two colors of bricks. Flemish-cross bond *(top)*, for example, alternates standard Flemish courses with courses consisting entirely of stretchers.

Flemish-spiral bond *(center)* bands the wall with diagonal lines of contrasting headers. Constructed of standard Flemish courses, the bond is laid so that the headers in successive courses are staggered one half their width beyond the headers in the course below, with every course staggered in the same direction.

Garden-wall bond *(bottom)* consists of modified Flemish courses, with three stretchers separating successive headers. In this example, a large diamond is created with rows of contrasting bricks centered over a single contrasting header. With each new course, the row of contrasting bricks is lengthened by a half brick for five rows; thereafter each row is shortened by a half brick until, with the ninth course, only a single header remains. For such dovetailing diamond patterns, a preliminary sketch helps you determine the proper placement of the header bricks that form the top, bottom and center of each of the diamonds.

On brick veneer, where the brickwork will be exposed on only one side, you can accentuate any of these decorative patterns by offsetting the contrasting bricks ½ to 1 inch from the face of the wall, thus creating a pattern in relief.

Treating Mortar Joints as Design Elements

Two decorative joints. The grapevine joint, top, popular in colonial America, includes a narrow groove that runs down the center of the joint. An hour or two after laying the bricks, shape the mortar, using a special ridged jointer. Fit the tool between the bricks, press it down firmly and draw it slowly along the mortar, first tooling the vertical joints, then the horizontal joints.

For a rustic effect, form a weeping joint—also called an extruded joint—by laying bricks with excess mortar *(bottom)*. Allow the mortar that squeezes out of the joints to cure undisturbed.

Laying Bricks in Relief

Mortaring offset brick. To lay one or more projecting bricks, throw a line of mortar along the preceding course, and pat the mortar flat with the back of your trowel *(top)*. Take care not to furrow the mortar, and remove any that spills over the edge of the course by trimming it away with the edge of the trowel.

Lay the next course, using a mason's rule to position the offset bricks. Build the wall up another course or two; then carefully trim all the joints between offset bricks and bricks laid flush with the original wall plane, using a trowel or a tuck pointer *(bottom)*. Leave these joints flush, and do not strike them to give them the concave or furrowed finish of ordinary joints.

A Quoined Corner: Relief for the Eye

1 **Laying the first offset course.** Raise the inner and outer walls to the same height on both sides of the corner. Working only on the outer wall, spread a bed of mortar across the vertical mortar joint nearest the corner; continue the line of mortar along the adjacent leg of the wall a distance of two brick lengths. Lay a corner brick,

offsetting it about ½ inch from both faces of the wall; use a folding mason's ruler as a guide. Lay a second brick end to end with the first. Check for horizontal alignment with a mason's level, first along the top of the bricks, then along their outer faces. Adjust them, if necessary, by tapping them with a trowel handle.

Lay a third brick at the corner, along the other leg of the wall (*below, right*). Set it flush with the first brick and check its horizontal alignment, using a mason's level first along the top and then along the outer faces, as above. Then check the height of this first offset course with a story pole, as shown on page 76.

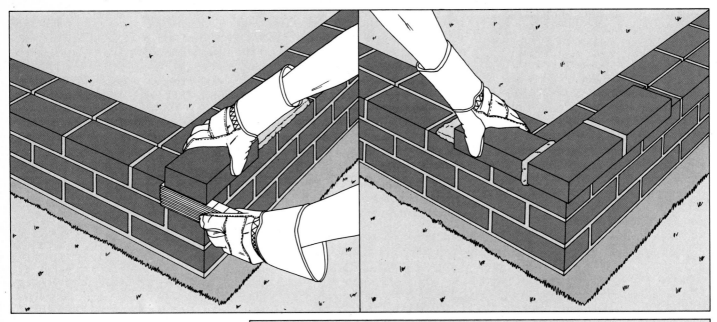

2 **Completing the first course of the lead.** With the first layer of offset bricks in place, begin a wall lead at this corner by laying three or four bricks down each leg of the wall. Set these bricks flush with the face of the wall, and furrow the mortar bed in which you lay them. Make their end joints slightly thicker than usual, to compensate for the quoin's ½-inch offset. Check both legs of this flush course with the level and the story pole.

To complete the corner, lay bricks along the inner wall, flush with the course below.

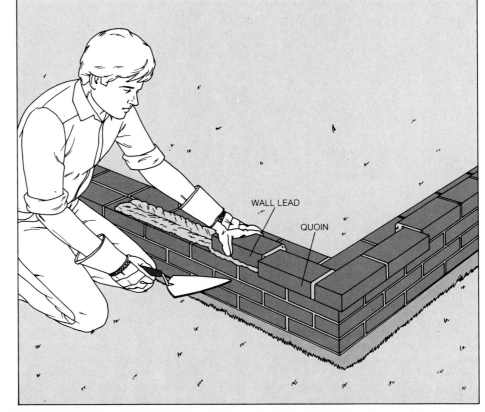

WALL LEAD

QUOIN

3 **Building up the quoin.** Lay a second course of offset bricks, using a half brick at the end of each leg so that the end bricks of the quoin line up with each other. Build the second course of the lead along both legs with bricks set flush with the wall surface. Begin these flush sections of lead with half bricks, and end them when the second course is a half brick short of the first course. Build a second course along the inner wall, as in Step 2.

Continue to lay courses of offset bricks until the quoin is the desired height—usually five courses. Follow the patterns of bricks established in the first two courses, and at every second course set metal wall ties *(page 84)* across the inner and outer walls to bind them together. At frequent intervals, check the offset and flush bricks for plumb and for horizontal alignment. Align each course with a story pole.

4 **Finishing the quoin.** When the quoin is five courses high, lay a course of bricks flush with the face of the wall. Begin the course with a brick spanning the vertical mortar joint nearest the corner, setting the brick ½ inch in from the faces of the quoin. Continue to lay bricks in this course, ending a half brick short of the previous course. Lay a second course of bricks in the same manner, but use furrowed mortar as for an ordinary wall. Then build up the inner thickness of wall to the level of these two courses.

Build a lead, either quoined or conventional, at the opposite end of the wall.

5 **Filling in the wall.** Run a mason's line between the first courses of the leads, anchoring the line near the quoin with a nail driven into the mortar. Attach the line similarly at the other lead, or fasten it to a mason's line and blocks fitted around the corners. Adjust the line to run even with the top of the course. Lay bricks in a dry run from lead to lead, spacing the bricks evenly. Then mortar down the bricks, using the mason's line as a guide. Lay a matching course of bricks along the inner surface of the wall.

Reposition the mason's line along the top of the next course, and continue to raise the wall in this fashion until it is even with the top recessed band of the quoin.

6 **Adding a second quoin.** Lay a course of offset bricks as in Step 1, beginning with a brick covering the vertical mortar joint nearest the corner. Since this joint now lies on the other leg of the wall, the positions of the long and short legs of the quoin will be reversed. Using the brick pattern set by these two courses, build up the second quoin and its lead as in Steps 2 through 5. Then fill in the intervening wall. Continue in this way, alternating quoins with recessed courses.

A Masonry Screen That Lets Air Circulate

Anatomy of a latticework wall. An 18-foot screen, long enough to add privacy to a patio or to conceal a carport, consists of two openwork brick panels, each about 7½ feet long, buttressed by three brick piers each a foot square. The panels, just one brick thick, are banded top and bottom by three courses of solid brickwork, to frame the lattice and add stability. The lattice bricks are spaced to leave open pockets. With 11 courses of latticework and 6 courses of solid brickwork, the wall is almost 4 feet high.

Like all brick walls, the screen rests on a concrete footing. In this example, the concrete slab is 8 inches thick and lies on a 6-inch bed of coarse gravel; the top of the slab is 1 inch below grade level. The slab is 16 inches wide, which allows for 2 inches of clearance on either side of the piers, and it projects 2 inches beyond the ends of the brickwork. In many areas, a footing of this design is adequate only for lightweight walls, no more than 4 feet high. Because of this, and because latticework masonry is fragile, limit your screen to the height shown.

Building a Brick Lattice

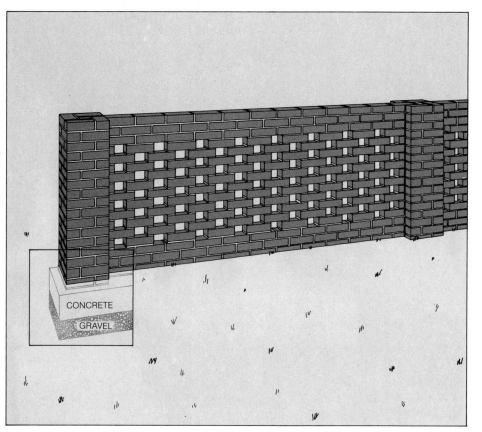

HALF BRICK

1 A dry run. Snap two chalk lines along the slab, 2 inches in from the edges of the slab and 12 inches apart; these lines will serve to mark the outer faces of the piers. Snap a second pair of lines, 4 inches apart and 4 inches in from the pier lines; these lines mark the outer faces of the panels. Measure off and mark where the piers will cross these lines, using an ordinary crayon or a builder's crayon to mark the concrete.

With the chalk lines and crayon marks as guides, lay bricks in a dry run for the bottom course. Begin with an end pier, pinwheeling the bricks around a center half brick in the arrangement shown, so that the first brick of the wall panel intersects the pier. Then lay bricks between the chalk lines to the middle pier. For a 7½-foot panel, 11 or 12 bricks should cover the distance. Space the mortar joints between the

bricks so that the last brick falls a mortar joint away from the pier mark or so that it falls halfway across the pier mark. Lay out the second pier, either in the same arrangement as for the first pier or as shown in the right inset, depending on the position of the final brick in the wall panel. Repeat the procedure for the second panel and the third pier, which should match one of the layouts shown in the insets.

105

2 **A band of solid brickwork.** Lay the first course of each pier in mortar, as well as the first two lead bricks at each end of one of the panels. Check the mortar bed for thickness with a story pole, and check the horizontal alignment of the bricks with a mason's level. Lay two more courses on the piers and the panel leads, alternating the arrangement of bricks on the pier so that the first bricks of the panel leads step back by a half brick on each course. Check your work frequently for alignment, plumb and course level.

Drive line pins or nails into the first mortar joints of the panel leads, and stretch a mason's line between them. Adjust the line to lie flush with the top of the first course. Use the line to fill in the intermediate bricks, removing three or four dry-run bricks at a time and replacing them in mortar. Lay the next two courses, then repeat the process for the second panel. Patch the holes left by the line pins with fresh mortar.

3 **Starting the latticework.** Do a dry run of the fourth course, beginning with the pier bricks. Where the pier is intersected by a panel brick, the intersecting brick must be cut by 2 inches before the rest of the course is laid. The resulting three-quarter brick is then set into the pier *(inset)*. Working from the two piers toward the center, fill in the panel bricks, leaving a space of about 4 inches between them; use the combined width of a header brick and a finger as a convenient space guide. When all the bricks are in place, check to make sure the spacing is even.

Set the pier bricks in mortar. Then remove and set the first three or four lead bricks at each end of the panel. Use a mortar bed only as long as the brick and carefully remove any excess mortar with a trowel. Check this openwork lead for alignment with a story pole and a mason's level.

4 **Building latticework leads.** Build up the two openwork leads with a second course of pier and panel bricks, positioning the latter to span the 4-inch gaps in the first openwork course. Mortar these bricks in place with small beds of mortar, placed on the ends of the bricks below. Repeat the process until the openwork leads are five courses high; tie them into the piers as needed with three-quarter bricks. As you go, check the leads frequently for level and for plumb with a mason's level and a story pole.

5 **Filling in the latticework.** Stretch a mason's line flush with the top of the first course of the openwork leads and use it as a guide to set the remaining bricks of that course. Raise the line to match the second course of the leads and fill in the second course of openwork, spanning the 4-inch gaps in the first. Continue to fill in the openwork until it is even with the tops of the leads, raising the mason's line with each new course. Patch the holes left by the line pins with fresh mortar. Then repeat the process to raise the second openwork panel to the same height.

Build six-course leads as in Step 4, then add six courses of openwork. Use a tuck pointer to trim away any mortar that has squeezed into the open spaces, leaving a flush finish (inset).

6 **Capping the screen.** Lay a dry run of a new course of solid brickwork along the top of the panels. Adjust the spacing of the mortar joints so that they are even, then build three-course leads of solid brickwork as in Step 2. Take care not to spill the mortar into the open spaces of the latticework as you lay mortar for the first course of the leads. Check the leads frequently for plumb and level, and use a story pole to make sure the three courses are of uniform thickness. Using a mason's line as a guide, fill in the solid brickwork between the leads.

A Wall with Serpentine Grace

Unlike the corrupting serpent in the Biblical Garden of Eden, a serpent-shaped, or serpentine, garden wall, meandering among flower beds and casting sinuous shadows, adds only grace and charm to its surroundings. Such a wall, however, presents unusual complexities of design and construction. Classical serpentine walls, following the design introduced to the United States from Europe by Thomas Jefferson, consist of a single thickness of bricks. Repeated S curves, rather than frequent piers and a double thickness of bricks, give these walls stability.

The S curves are a succession of arcs, each an identical segment from a circle of a given radius. The arcs are linked end to end in mirror image down the length of the wall; the proportions of the arcs determine the wall's inherent strength. The radius of the arcs should be no greater than twice the height of the wall, and the total sweep of the arcs from side to side should cover a distance equal to at least half the height of the wall.

Other design features add strength. Although you can have any number of S curves and can end the wall at any point along a curve, you ought to buttress the ends of the wall with brick piers that are at least 12 inches square. For additional reinforcement, set corrugated-steel wall ties *(page 84)* after every fifth course, running the ties lengthwise from brick to brick.

As with any wall, a solid footing is essential. For serpentine walls up to 4 feet high—a sensible maximum—a 14-inch gravel-and-concrete footing, resting at or above the frost line, is adequate. Ordinarily, you can simply dig a serpentine trench 16 inches wide and 4 inches longer than the wall, then pour in 6 inches of gravel, followed by 8 inches of concrete. In sandy soil, you may have to dig a wider trench and set up curved forms *(page 42)* to contain the concrete. In clay or in boggy ground, it may be necessary to excavate below the frost line; consult a building inspector about local soil conditions.

Use standard bricklaying techniques to build your wall: Lay buttered bricks in a furrowed bed of mortar, and make sure that the vertical mortar joints in successive courses are staggered. Since the curves of the wall will make it impossible for you to use the conventional stepped leads and mason's line to align the courses, you will have to employ other methods of checking the courses for plumb, level and proper curve.

A plywood template spanning two half arcs, center point to center point, serves as a pattern for keeping the curves of each new course aligned with the curves below. On each side of the wall, parallel string lines mark the outer sweep of the curves. The strings, stretched between stakes at least the height of the wall, are raised level with each course in turn. The string lines serve two purposes: They ensure that the wall is plumb at the outermost point of each curve and that all the outermost bricks along each course are at the same level. These outermost bricks can be used as reference points for leveling the intermediate bricks. Be scrupulous and thorough with all of these checks to avoid misaligning and thus weakening your wall.

Anatomy of a serpentine wall. This traditional serpentine wall consists of one thickness of bricks, built to a height of 4 feet. Each of its undulating curves is a segment of a circle with a radius of 6 feet. The distance between two parallel lines touching the outermost points of the curves is 3 feet 3½ inches. On each side of the wall, the distance between the outermost points of successive curves is 15 feet 10 inches. Brick piers 12 inches square buttress the ends of the wall, and steel wall ties running from brick to brick at every fifth course provide additional strength.

Just below ground level, the wall rests on a similarly curved concrete footing 16 inches wide, 8 inches thick and 2 inches longer than the wall at each end. To aid drainage, a 6-inch layer of gravel underlies the concrete.

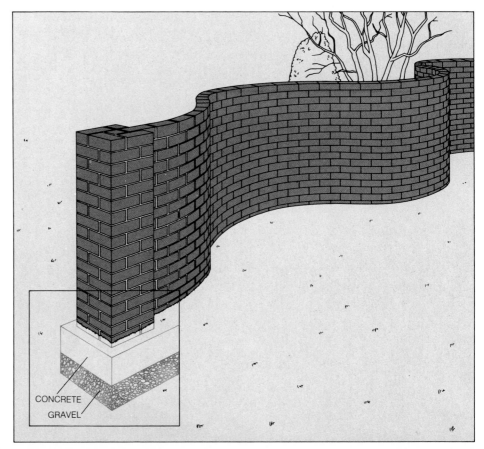

CONCRETE

GRAVEL

Laying the Groundwork for the Wall

1 **Tracing the template.** Rule a parallel base line 1 inch in from one of the long edges of a 4-by-8-foot sheet of ½-inch plywood. Attach one end of a length of picture wire to a stake or other fixed object. Measure out 6 feet from this center point, and twist the wire around a felt-tipped marker. Position the plywood so that the mark-er wire, stretched along one end of the plywood, extends 3 feet past the base line *(inset)*. With the wire taut, draw an arc across the plywood.

Reverse the plywood and adjust the sheet so that the wire runs parallel to the other end, 1 inch in from the edge, with the marker extending just to the base line. Draw an arc toward the center of the sheet, extending the curve until the two arcs touch. With a saber saw, cut along the marked lines to free the template from the waste *(inset)*, starting at the end of one arc and switching to the other arc at the point where the two touch each other.

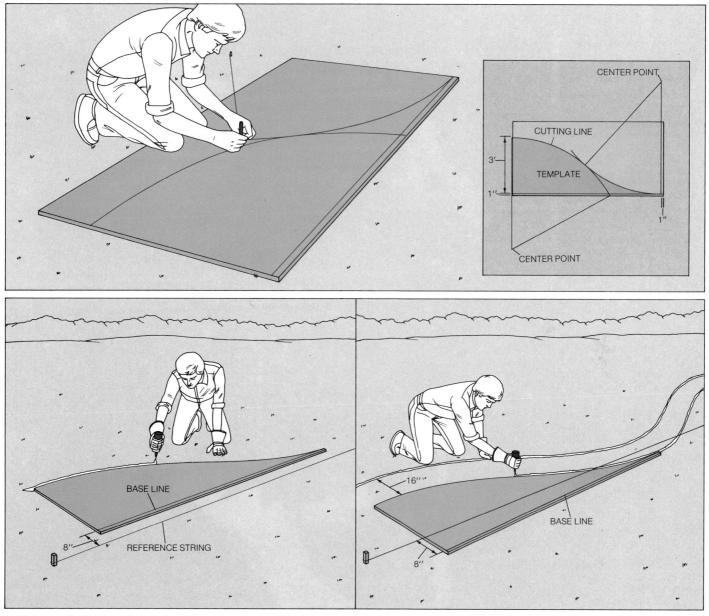

2 **Outlining the footing trench.** Stretch a reference string along a line representing the outermost curves of one face of the wall. Make the string slightly longer than the planned wall and secure it to two stakes, so that it lies about an inch above the ground. Position the template near one end of the string, with the ruled base line half the width of the planned trench away from the string—8 inches, in this case *(left)*. Outline the curved edge of the template with lime *(page 28)*. Then turn the template end over end, and mark off the desired number of serpentine curves. Outline a parallel serpentine by positioning the template's base line half the trench width away from the other side of the reference string *(right)*; when the outline is completed, the two curved lines should be separated by the full width of the trench—in this example, a total of 16 inches. Extend the curved lines at each end with straight, parallel lines about 14 inches long to mark the pier footings.

Remove the reference string and dig a footing trench between the lines you have marked with lime. Pour a footing as shown on pages 40-45, and allow it to cure for at least 24 hours before beginning to lay bricks for the wall.

3 **Setting reference lines.** Mark the outermost curves for both faces of the wall with a pair of parallel strings. First, outline one wall face on the footing, using the template. Place the curved edge of the template 6 inches in from one edge of the footing, and draw a crayon line along it, turning the template end over end as in Step 2; allow 14 inches at each end of the footing for piers. Use a framing square to trace a 12-inch square for each pier, leaving a 2-inch margin around the outline.

Stretch a string lengthwise along the footing at ground level so that it touches successive outermost curves along the crayon line. Extend the string 2 or 3 feet beyond each end of the footing and attach it to 5-foot reference poles, carefully plumbed and driven firmly into the ground. Stretch a second string across the footing, parallel to the first string and 3 feet 3½ inches away from it; this marks the farthest sweep of the other side of the wall. Bricks positioned at the apexes of the curves will help you check the position of the strings.

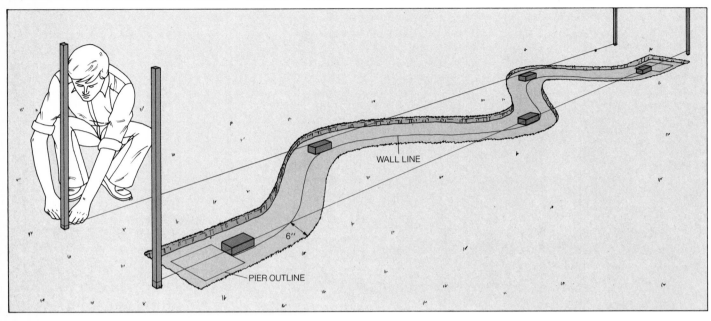

WALL LINE

6″

PIER OUTLINE

Raising the Wall

1 **Laying a dry run.** Using a story pole as a guide (page 76), raise the two strings between the reference poles the height of one course above the footing. Lay a dry course of bricks inside one pier outline; then lay a course of bricks down the center of the footing, aligning them with the crayon line that marks one face of the wall. Set the bricks about a finger's width apart to allow for mortar joints. When you reach the opposite pier outline, adjust the spacing between the last few bricks so that the final brick either falls a mortar joint short of the outline or overlaps the outline at the brick's midpoint (page 105). Then lay a dry course of bricks for the pier, using half bricks, if necessary, to interlock properly with the wall.

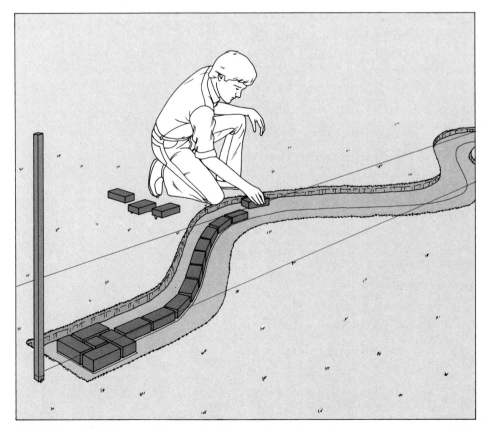

2 **Checking for alignment.** Lay the first course of bricks in mortar, beginning at a pier and working down the serpentine in a three-step sequence: Remove three or four bricks at a time, throw and furrow a line of mortar, butter the bricks and replace them. Be sure the tops of the outermost bricks along a curve align with the reference strings marking the course level; then check the intermediate bricks for course level by spanning a section of curve with a 6-foot length of straight 2-by-4 board, topped by a mason's level secured by tape. Position the board so that one end of it rests on an outermost brick for reference. To bring bricks into alignment, tap them with a trowel handle to lower them; or remove them and add more mortar to raise them.

Add a second course, moving the reference string to the new course level. At the piers, use brick arrangements that place the vertical joints at the midpoint of the bricks in the course below.

3 **Checking for consistent curves.** As you lay each course, set the plywood template into the curves of the brickwork, and look down on it from above. Make sure that each end of the template touches a brick at the outermost points of the curve; then bring the intermediate bricks into alignment by tapping them with the trowel handle until they lie against the template's curved edge. Repeat the process along the length of the wall, flipping the template as necessary to match the serpentine curves.

4 **Adding to the brickwork.** Continue raising the wall, course by course, resetting the string lines for each course and checking each completed course for level, plumb and curvature. After every fifth course, set a steel wall tie across each vertical joint before you throw the mortar for the next course. As the wall rises, you may need to stand on a stepladder and have a pair of helpers hold the template in place while you check the curvature. Build the wall and piers to a height of 18 courses of brick—4 feet.

Understanding the Principles of the Brick Arch

The structural purpose of an arch is to span an opening and support the weight of the masonry above it. In a brick arch, mortar holds the bricks together, but gravity is what actually holds them in place. Either the mortar joints or the bricks themselves have to be slightly wedge-shaped so that the weight of the load upon the wedges forces the bricks tightly together. The arch then conveys its load onto the supporting walls.

Arches have been a popular architectural feature for many centuries, but in modern masonry they are more frequently built for the beauty of their form than for their structural advantages. In brick veneer, for example, an arch supports only a small section of bricks directly above it. Whatever its purpose, the arch must be properly proportioned and carefully built in order to last.

Four traditional arch shapes—semicircular, segmental, elliptical and pointed—are commonly used today to span the openings for doors and windows. Construction techniques for the semicircular arch are shown on pages 113-116. The same techniques can be used to build the other three shapes, but the design and structural planning are somewhat more complicated than for a semicircle. For each of these shapes, the necessary geometry is provided in a diagram next to an illustration of the finished arch.

A fifth design, the flat or jack arch shown on page 118, does not look like an arch at all. It is, however, built on the same principle as the other four styles in that its pieces wedge together to hold themselves in place. Although jack arches can be built to be self-supporting, they are usually constructed on top of L-shaped steel lintels.

The lintel for a jack arch should span the opening and extend 8 inches onto the walls to each side. Lintel sizes are designated by the length of their flanges: A lintel 3½ by 3½ inches is sufficient for openings of 6 feet or less.

Although an arch may not serve a larger structural purpose, it does have to be self-supporting. Consequently, any arch, regardless of its shape, should have a face height at least as great as the thickness of the wall surrounding it, and its depth should equal the thickness of the wall. Structural considerations also limit the distance an arch can safely span. Do not undertake to build an arch more than 5 feet wide. Although an arch can span a distance greater than this, such a project should be left to an experienced mason.

With the exception of the jack arch, all arches are constructed with the aid of temporary shoring called the buck or centering. For brick arches, the buck can be built with ½-inch plywood and 2-by-4s. The buck serves as a template while the bricks are being laid and carries the load of the arch until the mortar sets. The buck should stay in place for 5 to 10 days after the arch is completed.

There are two general methods of building brick arches. One method is to use standard bricks and shape the mortar joints; the alternative is to use specially shaped bricks so that the joints can be uniform. Shaped bricks, custom-cut at the factory to your specifications, are available in sets from masonry suppliers. Such bricks generally produce a better-looking arch, but they cost more.

If you do choose to order factory-shaped bricks, supply a full-sized drawing of the arch. Also, plan the project well in advance, because delivery of the bricks will likely be slow. A full-sized drawing is a useful idea in any event, since it eliminates mistakes in planning and facilitates construction of the buck.

Before starting on an arch, build corner leads for the surrounding masonry. Position the leads far enough from the opening so as not to obstruct the construction of the arch, and carry them to the planned height of the arch.

●

Arch-builders' jargon. Common terms used to describe the parts of an arch are labeled on the brick arch at right, along with the measurements used to plot its shape. The curved inner edge of the arch is called its intrados; the curved edge at top is the extrados. The undersurface of the arch is the soffit. The masonry walls that support an arch are called abutments. The inclined surfaces of the abutments on which the arch rests are called skewbacks. Each wedge-shaped unit—brick or brick and mortar—is referred to as a voussoir.

The imaginary horizontal line between the points where the arch meets the vertical sides of the abutments is called the spring line. The rise of an arch is the vertical distance from the spring line to the center of the intrados. The distance between the abutments is the span of the arch.

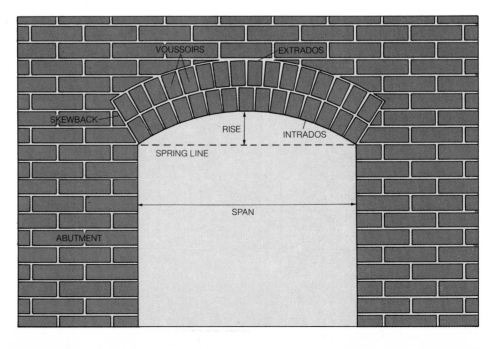

Spanning an Opening with a Half Circle

Anatomy of a semicircular arch. This example of a semicircular arch consists of two rings of standard-sized bricks laid in a rowlock header pattern (*page 89*). To support such an arch, the abutments must be two bricks thick. For the bricks to follow the curve of the arch, the mortar joints must be made slightly wedge-shaped—thicker at the top than at the bottom. Because the outside ring follows a wider radius than the inside ring, it requires a greater number of bricks.

The shape of this arch provides great strength because the weight of the bricks in the arch, as well as the weight of the masonry above it, is carried downward onto the abutments.

Constructing an Arch with Standard-Sized Bricks

1 **Shaping the buck.** On a sheet of ½-inch plywood, draw a spring line for the arch several inches in from the edge. Drive a nail at the center of the line and use the nail to swing an arc, with wire and a pencil, connecting the ends of the line as described on page 109. At the end of the spring line, mark a perpendicular line running to the edge of the plywood. Then, with a saber saw, cut along the line and around the arc.

Using this piece of plywood as a pattern, cut a matching piece. Nail 2-by-4 spacer blocks on edge between the two plywood pieces to hold them apart. Position one long spacer along the spring line and shorter pieces at intervals around the curved edge, fanning out from the center like the spokes of a wheel.

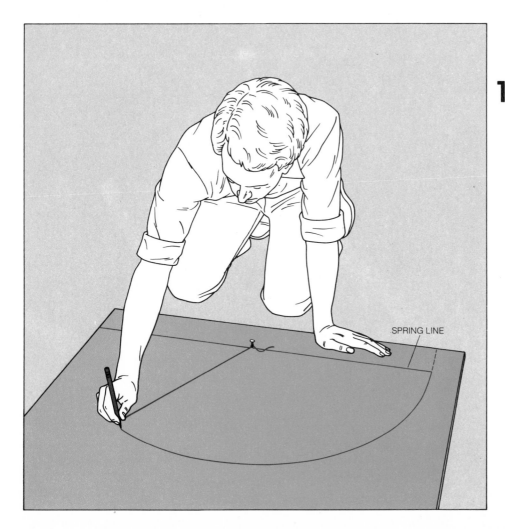

SPRING LINE

2 **Marking brick positions.** With the buck laid flat on the ground, assemble an odd number of bricks on end around the curved edge, starting ⅜ inch above the spring line. Space the bricks ⅜ inch apart, and position one brick exactly in the center of the arch; if necessary, increase the gaps between the other bricks to fill out the curve evenly. Mark all the brick positions on the face of the buck.

Arrange a second ring of bricks around the first, leaving a ⅜-inch gap between rings. Start ⅜ inch above the spring line, and space the bricks evenly around this second ring. Note the spacing by marking a stick to show the width at both ends of the wedge-shaped gaps. Then use this stick as a gauge when you go on to build the outside ring of the arch.

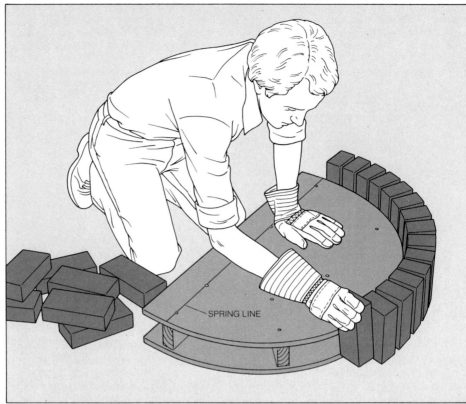

SPRING LINE

3 **Setting up the buck.** Use double-headed nails to attach 2-by-4 legs between the plywood faces of the buck, then brace the legs with a 2-by-4 crosspiece on each side. To determine the length of the legs, hold the buck in place in the arch opening, with the spring line level with the tops of the abutments, while a helper measures the distance between the spring-line spacer block and the ground. Check the length of the legs by propping the buck in place before driving the nails. Cut the crosspieces equal in length to the span of the arch.

Raise the buck into the opening, hold a carpenter's level across the top edges of the two plywood pieces and, if necessary, slide shims beneath the legs to make the buck sit perfectly level. The plywood edges should lodge snugly between the abutments. If the buck tends to tip, drive a masonry nail through each leg into mortar joints at the sides of the opening.

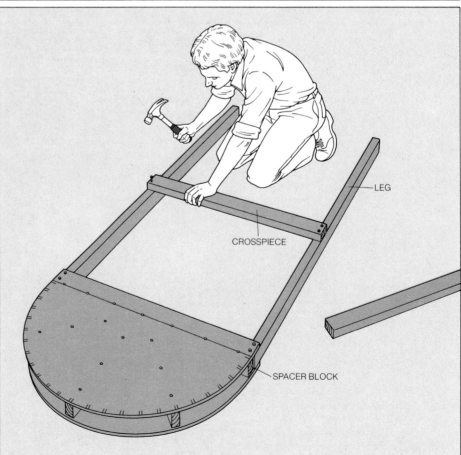

LEG

CROSSPIECE

SPACER BLOCK

4 **Beginning the soffit.** To butter bricks for the inside ring of the arch, settle mortar firmly on the blade of your trowel by shaking the loaded blade sharply downward. Then scrape mortar along three edges of one bed side of a brick *(below, left)*, leaving clear the edge that will face down into the opening. Lay the first brick atop the corner of the abutment; make sure its soffit face is resting squarely against the buck. Use the handle of the trowel to tamp the brick into the mortar *(below, right)* until it fits precisely between the marks on the buck.

Continue laying bricks in this manner until you reach the marks that you made on the buck to position the center brick; then go back and build up the other side of the arch. As you work, raise a mason's line as a guide in aligning the front ends of the arch bricks.

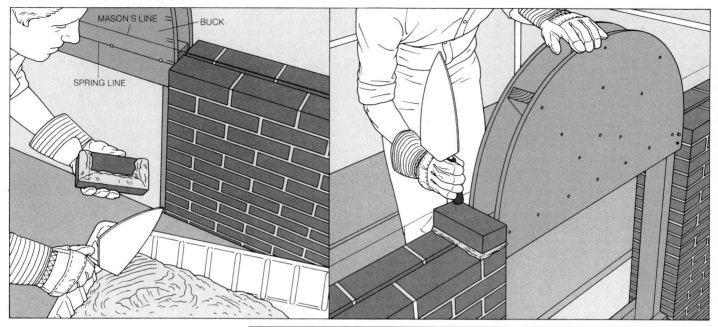

5 **Laying the center brick.** Butter the last brick on both bed sides, using the technique shown in Step 4. Use the blade of the trowel to shape the mortar so that it tapers slightly toward the soffit face of the brick. Slide the brick into place, tapping it with the trowel handle to wedge it against the buck.

When the mortar has hardened partially, finish all of the joints that will be visible on the completed arch *(page 79)*. Cut a section of steel joint-reinforcement wire long enough to fit over the top of the arch. Bend the wire to lie flat along the top of the first ring of bricks, and lay it in place.

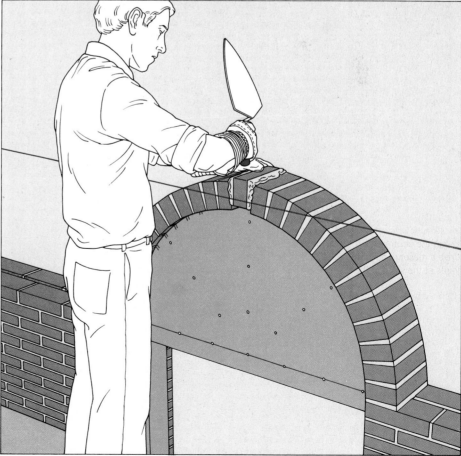

6 Building the outside ring. For the second ring, butter one bed side of each adjoining brick on all four edges, but spread the mortar thicker at the top than at the bottom. Also spread mortar on the brick face that will lie against the inside ring. Start laying bricks from the abutment corners, working toward the center. Tap each brick into the mortar until there is a ⅜-inch mortar joint between the rings of bricks.

When you are partway up the curve of the arch, you can simplify the job by throwing lines of bed mortar along the top of the inside ring; in this way you will only need to butter one bed side of each subsequent brick. Pay close attention to the spacing between bricks in the outside ring so that the last bricks will fit when you reach the center. Use the stick gauge made in Step 2 as a guide in shaping these joints.

7 Adding masonry above the arch. Fill in horizontal courses of masonry around the arch, cutting bricks diagonally to meet the curve of the arch. To make a neat diagonal cut, mark the cutting line with a pencil and a ruler on the outer face of the brick; then score the line ½ inch deep, using a circular saw fitted with a masonry blade. Finish the cut by chipping away the waste portion of the brick with the blade end of a bricklayer's hammer. Continue raising courses on both sides until the arch is fully enclosed.

After the mortar has completely cured, in about five days, carefully disassemble the buck and its supports. Remove the crosspieces first; then, with a helper supporting the buck, remove the nails that fasten the legs and pry the bottoms of the 2-by-4s toward the center of the opening. Ease the buck out from under the arch.

8 Repointing the soffit. With a cold chisel and a light sledge hammer, cut out the hardened mortar from the joints of the soffit, clearing them to a depth of ½ inch. Then, using the back of a trowel as a palette, hold a fresh batch of mortar up close to the cleared joints and force new mortar into them with a tuck pointer. Fill the joints completely. Then, when the mortar has partially hardened, finish the soffit joints to match those on the face of the arch.

A Gallery of Classic Arches

A segmental arch. The shape of this shallow arch, a segment of a large circle, imposes considerable sideways thrust on its abutments, which must be substantial enough to withstand it. A segmental arch would not, for example, be built between unsupported piers or columns. The rise of a segmental arch is arbitrary, but for structural reasons it must be between one twelfth and one fourth the span.

The geometry used to design a segmental arch and to shape its buck is diagramed at right, below. Line AB is the span of the arch; line CD is the rise and is extended below line AB to provide a vertical center line for the arch. Using point B as a center and BD as a radius, swing an arc *(shown here in gray)*. Then use point D as the center and DB as the radius to swing a second arc, intersecting the first. The intersections of

the arcs establish points E and F. Draw a line through E and F that intersects the vertical center line, thus establishing point G. With point G as your center and GA as radius, swing an arc between points A and B to mark the intrados of the arch. Then extend the radius by the planned face height of the arch and swing a second arc, again using G as the center; this arc will mark the extrados.

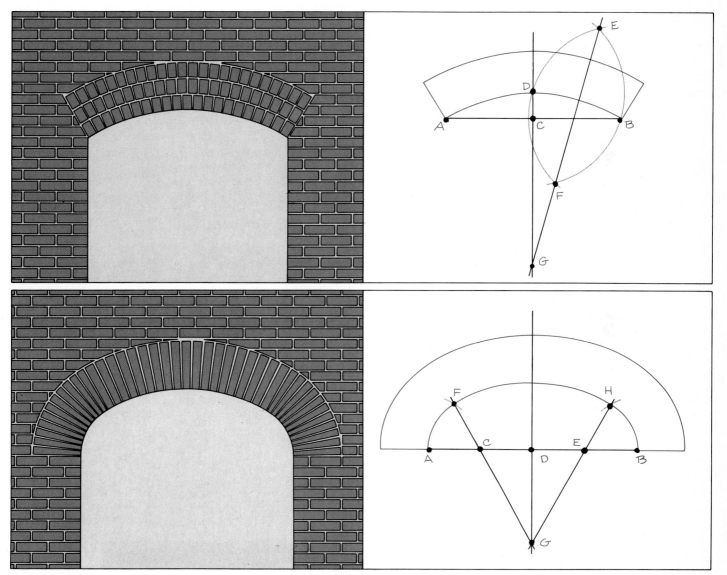

An elliptical arch. The shape of most elliptical arches, like the one at left, above, is actually an approximation of a true elliptical curve. Such a shape is drawn from three centers, as shown in the diagram at right, above, resulting in less rise than a true ellipse. This makes the arch suitable for spanning relatively wide openings without extending high into the wall above. The example shown here is constructed of factory-shaped bricks assembled in a soldier course.

To draw this elliptical arch, divide the span of the arch (shown here as line AB) into four equal parts, thus establishing points C, D and E. Using point C as a center and CA as a radius, swing an arc that intersects line AB. Using the same radius but point A as the center, swing a second arc, intersecting the first arc at point F. Repeat this procedure, using the same radius and points E and B as centers, to establish point H. Draw a vertical center line through point D;

then extend lines through points F and C, and points H and E, intersecting the center line at point G. Using G as a center and GF as the radius, swing an arc to connect points F and H.

The three arcs—A to F, F to H and H to B— make up the intrados of the arch. Then, using the same three centers (C, E and G), draw a line to mark the extrados, extending each radius by the face height of the arch.

A pointed arch. This example of a pointed arch is built with wedge-shaped bricks arranged in a soldier course culminating at the peak of the arch; the mortar joints are uniform in width. The shape of the arch is a variation on a true Gothic arch, which is much more pointed and rises higher into the wall above. When drawn as shown in the diagram at right, below, the rise of the arch is arbitrary.

To design a pointed arch, mark line AB equal to the span of the arch. At the center of line AB, establish point C; then draw CD equal to the desired rise. Draw a line connecting points A and D. From the center of line AD, draw a perpendicular line, intersecting line AB at point E. Measure the distance from point E to point B, and mark point F equidistant from point A. Using point E as a center and EA as a radius, swing an arc from A to D to mark one side of the intrados. Repeat, using F as the center and FB as radius, for the other side of the intrados. Use the same centers—F and E—for the extrados, but increase the radius by the face height of the arch.

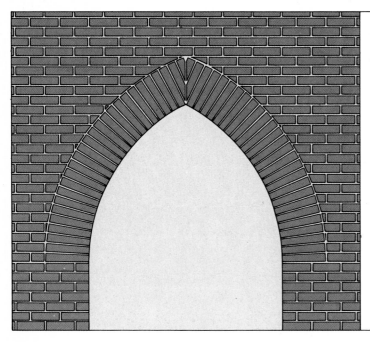

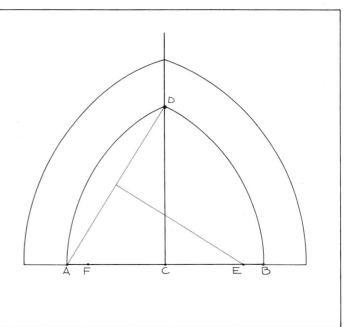

An Arch That Takes the Place of a Stone Lintel

Anatomy of a jack arch. A flat arch is called a jack arch. Each brick in the arch is cut to a slightly different shape, because each sits at a slightly different angle to the steel lintel. When ordering a set of bricks for a jack arch, be prepared to specify the span of the opening, the thickness of the mortar joints you will be using, and the height of the arch in terms of horizontal courses of surrounding brick (four, in this example). Also specify the angle of the skewback (generally 70°), the depth of the soffit, and the pattern of the brickwork in the face of the arch—a bonded pattern in this arch.

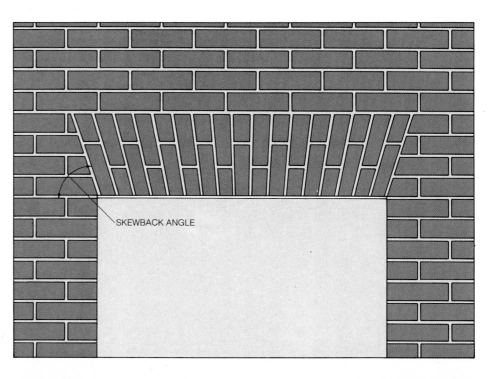

SKEWBACK ANGLE

Creating a Jack Arch with Factory-Shaped Bricks

1 Making the pattern. Cut a full-sized pattern for the arch from a piece of ¼-inch plywood, and lay all of the arch bricks in place on the pattern. Leave spaces for mortar joints between the bricks, including joints at either end of the pattern. Since factory-made arch sets are crated in the exact order in which they are to be assembled, take care to arrange the pieces in the same configuration in which they were shipped.

When all of the bricks are in place, mark the positions of the mortar-joint gaps along the top and bottom edges of the pattern. Then remove the bricks, again working in exactly the order in which they were assembled.

2 Framing the arch. Raise courses of bricks to the planned height of the arch on both sides of the opening. For the first course above the spring line, lay the end bricks no closer than 8 inches from the sides of the opening. Offset each succeeding course one half brick farther.

Install a steel lintel as described on page 87, Step 1. Scrape a little mortar off a trowel onto the front edge of the lintel, where it rests on the abutments, to hide the ends of the lintel.

3 **Positioning the skewback bricks.** Add bricks
to the courses installed in Step 2 until the ends of
each course extend far enough over the top of
the opening to be covered by the plywood pattern
when it is held in place above the opening. For
the first course, simply lay bricks mortarless on
top of the lintel, leaving ⅜-inch mortar-joint
gaps between the brick ends. Lay a mortar bed
between the courses above, but again leave
the vertical joints free of mortar. Step each succeeding course farther back from the center
of the opening, as in Step 2.

4 **Marking the skewback angle.** Align the bottom of the plywood pattern with the top edge of
the lintel, and center the pattern in the opening. Mark the skewback bricks with slanted pencil
lines, following the sides of the pattern. Number the marked bricks from bottom to top, then
remove all of the bricks that were installed in
Step 3; scrape off any mortar that adheres to the
surfaces. Cut the marked bricks, following the
procedures shown on page 116, Step 7.

5 **Building the skewbacks.** Return the numbered and cut bricks to their original positions and mortar them permanently in place. Rest the plywood pattern on the lintel as you install each brick; tamp the brick into the mortar until it fits flush against the edge of the pattern.

Use chalk to transfer the joint marks on the pattern to the backup wall behind the arch and to the front lip of the steel lintel. Stretch a mason's line even with the tops of the skewbacks.

6 **Beginning the arch.** Butter three edges of one bed side of the bottom corner brick of the arch; do not spread mortar on the edge that will rest on the lintel. Then lay the corner brick in place against the skewback. With the handle of the trowel, tamp the brick into the mortar until its bottom end is lined up with the marks on the lintel. Lay mortar on the top end of this first brick, then butter the half brick that fits on top of it. Tamp the half brick in place, aligning its top with the mason's line and its sides with the marks on the backup wall. Install the first two bricks at the other end of the arch in the same way.

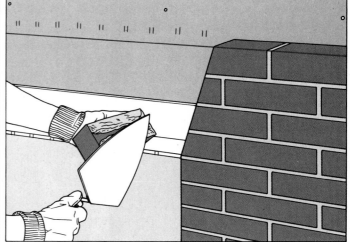

7 **Completing the job.** Fill in the remaining bricks of the arch, working from both sides toward the center. Keep the arch pieces carefully organized so that you never lose the configuration worked out by the brick manufacturer. Pay close attention to the thickness of the mortar joints, fitting each piece squarely between its marks; otherwise the center pieces will not fit. When you get to the center, butter the middle bricks on both sides and tap them into place with the handle of the trowel.

To reinforce the top of the arch, lay a row of wall ties, end to end, in the mortar bed for the first course of bricks above the arch.

Stone Arches Built to Carry Their Own Weight

The soaring stone arches of centuries-old cathedrals and aqueducts give ample testimony to the strength, grace and durability of this simple form. Replaced in most modern construction by more economical concrete, the stone arch can nevertheless lend a touch of timelessness to any setting, spanning windows, doors, fireplaces—even standing by itself on a pair of piers to frame an entryway.

The principles and procedures for building a stone arch closely parallel those used for the brick arches shown on the preceding pages. However, the greater complexities of measuring and cutting stone make the work more exacting, and you will probably need a helper to position the heavier stones. You may also require scaffolding on each side of the wall to provide convenient positions for both workers.

Like a brick arch, a stone arch is only as strong as its abutments and foundation footing, to which it transmits downward and outward pressures. The foundation footing between the abutments must be continuous, to prevent the abutments from slipping, sinking or turning independently. The abutments—whether they are walls or freestanding piers (pages 90-93)—must have at least 24 hours for their mortar to set before arch stones are laid between them. The piers for an arch that is not part of a larger wall ought to be at least 12 inches thick, as should the arch itself.

Stones for an arch, like those for a wall, must be strong and weather resistant; but they should also be workable, since you will need to do a lot of precise shaping (pages 10-14). Although single stones that match the thickness of the wall produce the strongest arch, they may be too heavy to handle. Smaller stones can be used in twos or threes to make up the requisite thickness without affecting the strength unduly. You may even want to use a combination of stones to produce an arch slightly thicker than the wall, so that the protruding outer faces will highlight the arch.

For very precise cuts, take your stone and a template of the arch to a professional stonemason with facilities for cutting stones of the size you are using. If you make the template from ½-inch plywood, you can later use it as part of the buck needed for building the arch.

The buck for a stone arch is similar to that used for a brick arch (page 113), but it is thicker because the wall is thicker. The 2-by-4 spacers are 1 inch shorter than the wall thickness, and they are positioned with their grain running perpendicular to the wall. In the case of a curved arch, the buck is covered with a strip of hardboard to hold the mortar in place until it sets. Because of the great weight of stone, the buck is supported by four 4-by-4 posts, one at each corner. Wooden shims wedge the buck into place, and after the arch is built, removing the shims relieves the compression on the buck assembly. It is then easy to pull out the cross-braced supports and lower the buck.

Use the same semidry portland-cement mortar for a stone arch as for a stone wall (page 90). Cut the stones to allow for uniform mortar joints ½ to ¾ inch wide, and after the arch is built, strike the joints to match the joint depths of the arch abutments. For maximum safety, allow time for the mortar to cure completely—it takes about 10 days—before you remove the buck.

A Peaked Arch from Two Stone Slabs

TRIANGULAR BUCK
SPREADER
SHIM

1 Setting up the buck. Make a triangular buck with the desired span and rise (Step 1, page 113) and position it in the opening, using wedge-shaped shims to adjust it to the proper height. Support the buck with cross-braced 4-by-4 posts cut ½ inch shorter than the height of the spring line. Brace the posts firmly against the abutments with 2-by-4 spreaders, top and bottom. Insert long wooden shims between the top of each post and the buck. Tap the shims inward, working alternately on one and then the other, until the buck is raised to the spring line and is leveled. Using double-headed nails, fasten the pieces together by toenailing through the tops of the posts and the shims into the buck.

2 **Setting the skewback stones.** Make a skewback atop each abutment by selecting or cutting stones to span the thickness of the wall, slanting one end of each stone to form an approximate right angle with the top of the buck. Lay each skewback stone in a ¾-inch bed of mortar, with its angled end 1 inch away from the abutment edge. Let the mortar set for 24 hours or more.

3 **Mitering the lintel stones.** To measure the angled cuts for the peak of the lintel, hold a mason's level at the apex of the buck, perpendicular to the ground, and set the arms of a T bevel flush with the buck and the level. To determine the length of each lintel stone, measure the distance from the apex to the bottom of the skewback; allow for a ½-inch mortar joint at each end.

Select a paving stone at least 4 inches thick for each lintel; mark the length and the angled cut on the stones. Cut the stones (page 13), taking care not to cut them too short. Lay the lintels in place on top of the buck to check their fit. Remove the stones and trim them if necessary.

4 **Laying the lintels.** Throw a ¾-inch bed of mortar on the skewback of one abutment, and dampen the first lintel with water. With a helper, lower the stone into place, sliding it down the buck until the end rests in the mortar. Shift the lintel from side to side to center it on the buck, while continuing to press it against the mortar until the joint is ½ inch thick. Set the other lintel in the same way, then use a ½-inch tuck pointer to tamp mortar into the joint at the apex.

Allow the mortar to set for at least 24 hours. Then build the wall in level courses over the arch, beveling the stones adjacent to the lintel for a close fit (*inset*). Remove the buck after 10 days, then repoint and strike the joints on the underside of the lintel as shown on page 93.

A Semicircular Arch Made from Shaped Stones

1 **Building the buck.** Make a semicircular buck (*page 113*) with a span ½ inch less than the span between the abutments. Cut a strip of ¼-inch hardboard as wide as the thickness of the buck, and nail it over the arch of the buck, starting at one end and bending the hardboard gently as you fasten it to the edges of the plywood. At the opposite end, cut away any excess hardboard.

Lay the buck on its side and drive a nail at the center of the spring line. Cut a marking string about 18 inches longer than the radius of the arch, and attach the string to the nail.

2 **Prefitting the stones.** Select stones for the ends of the arch, preferably single stones as thick as the wall and of similar size. Position them at the ends of the buck, with one side flush against the arch. Pull the marking string taut over the bottom edge of one stone, and scratch a cutting line with a nail or a tuck pointer. Mark the other edge of the stone in the same way. Then mark both edges of the stone at the other end of the buck. Cut the stones along the lines *(page 12)*. You may also need to remove projections from the bottom faces of the stones so that they lie close to the curve of the buck.

Mark lines on the buck corresponding to the cutting lines on the top edges of the first pair of stones. Remove the stones and use the lines on the buck as references for marking the bottom edges of another pair, but leave gaps of ½ to ¾ inch between adjacent stones for mortar joints. Continue marking and cutting pairs of stones on opposite sides of the buck, working toward the top. Plan the stones so that they are nearly equal in size, and allow for a single keystone of similar size at the top of the buck. When the layout is complete, mark the stones with numbers to indicate their positions for assembly.

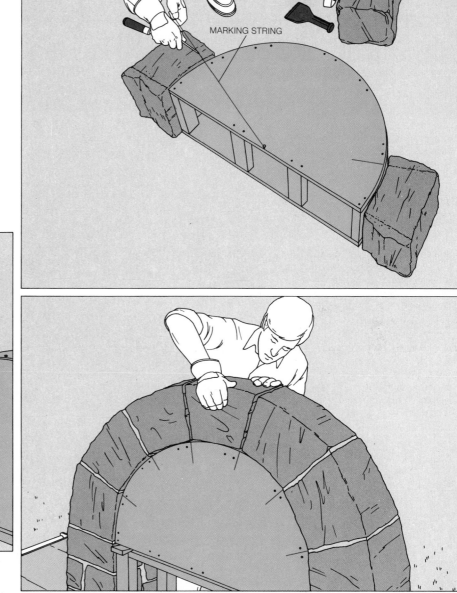

MARKING STRING

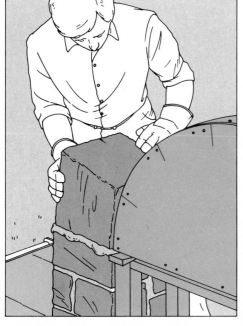

3 **Laying the stones.** Position the buck in the opening *(page 122)*, then lay a ¾-inch bed of mortar on one abutment. Dampen the first stone slightly and position it on the mortar bed, centering it on the buck. Twist or rock the stone lightly until it presses the mortar to a ½-inch joint; remove the excess mortar with a trowel.

Set the stone on the opposite abutment in the same manner. Then lay successive pairs of stones until only the gap for the keystone remains.

4 **Setting the keystone.** Slide the keystone, without mortar, into the space at the top of the arch, centering it carefully on the buck and between the adjacent stones. Add water to mortar until it is the consistency of a very thick paste, then load the mortar on the back of a trowel and use a ½-inch tuck pointer to pack mortar into the gaps between the keystone and adjacent stones. Use the same mortar mixture to strike all accessible joints *(page 93)*.

Let the mortar cure for 10 days, then remove the buck. Repoint the underside of the arch by cutting a ½-inch recess at each joint with a cold chisel. Then finish the joints to match the pattern of the rest of the arch.

Picture Credits

The sources for the illustrations in this book are shown below. The drawings were created by Jack Arthur, Roger Essley, Chuck Forsythe, William J. Hennessy Jr., John Jones, Dick Lee, John Martinez and Joan McGurren.

Cover: Fil Hunter. 6: Fil Hunter. 8, 9: William J. Hennessy Jr. from A and W Graphics. 11-15: Elsie J. Hennig. 16-19: Arezou Katoozian from A and W Graphics. 20-25: Frederic F. Bigio from B-C Graphics. 26: Fil Hunter. 28-33: Arezou Katoozian from A and W Graphics. 34-39: Edward L. Cooper. 41-45: Elsie J. Hennig. 46-50: Snowden Associates, Inc. 51: Ambrose M. Richardson, F.A.I.A., for the International Masonry Institute, Washington, D.C. 53-59: Walter Hilmers Jr. from HJ Commercial Art. 61: Frederic F. Bigio from B-C Graphics. 62, 63: John Massey. 65: Frederic F. Bigio from B-C Graphics. 66, 67: Frederic F. Bigio from B-C Graphics, inset renderings, Roger Essley. 68-71: Frederic F. Bigio from B-C Graphics. 72: Fil Hunter. 74-83: Eduino J. Pereira from Arts and Words. 85-89: Wagner/Graphic Design. 90-93: Walter Hilmers Jr. from HJ Commercial Art. 95-111: John Massey. 112-121: Frederic F. Bigio from B-C Graphics. 122-125: William J. Hennessy Jr. from A and W Graphics.

Acknowledgments

The index/glossary for this book was prepared by Louise Hedberg. The editors wish to thank the following: Kent Abraham, ABS Group, Washington, D.C.; Wayne S. Adaska, P.E., Energy and Water Resources Department, Portland Cement Association, Skokie, Ill.; American Institute of Architects, Washington, D.C.; Brick Institute of America, McLean, Va.; Peter Cleland, Clinton, Md.; Donald B. Corner, Assistant Professor of Architecture, Department of Architecture, University of Oregon, Eugene, Ore.; Cornelius Crouch, Arlington Public Schools Career Center, Arlington, Va.; Patrick Cullinane, Potomac, Md.; Maureen Cunningham, Editor, Brick Institute of America, McLean, Va.; John Duvall, Del Ray Tool Rental, Alexandria, Va.; Doug Ensminges, Arlington, Va.; Walter E. Galanty Jr., National Association of Brick Distributors, McLean, Va.; John Garms, Takoma Park, Md.; Dr. Robert Johnston, Dean, Rochester Institute of Technology, Rochester, N.Y.; Knute Jones, Grabber Washington, Landover, Md.; Dave Kimstall, AEG Power Tools, Norwich, Conn.; Charles Miller, Rawl—The Rawl Plug Co., Landover, Md.; Jay Morgan, Arlington, Va.; Office of Folklife Programs, Smithsonian Institution, Washington, D.C.; Scott Olin, Manager, Industrial Market, Rawl—The Rawl Plug Co., New Rochelle, N.Y.; Oriental Institute, University of Chicago, Chicago, Ill.; James C. Pan, Structural Engineer, Department of Building and Mechanical Inspections, City Hall, Alexandria, Va.; David Rhodes, Laurel, Md.; James H. Rockwell, Technical Director, International Institute of Housing Technology, California State University, Fresno, Calif.; Pete Sands, Star Expansion Co., Phoenix, Ariz.; Dr. Robert Scranton, Decatur, Ga.; Milton Shinberg, ABS Group, Washington, D.C.; L. C. Smith, Inc., Alexandria, Va.; Z. A. Snipes, Brick Institute of America, Atlanta, Ga.; John Taylor, Southeast Wrecking Company, Bel Alton, Md.; George L. Timm, Product Training Director, Star Expansion Co., Mountainville, N.Y.; WACO Ladder & Scaffolding Co., Brentwood, Md. The editors would also like to thank William King, a writer, for his assistance with this volume.

Index/Glossary

Included in this index are definitions of many of the masonry terms used in this book. Page references in italics indicate an illustration of the subject mentioned.

Abrasive saw, 16, *19*

Adobe bricks: adding emulsified asphalt, 68; casting stabilized bricks, 68, *69;* curing, 68, *69;* mixing mud, 68, *69;* mortar, 68; testing soil, 68

Aggregate: in concrete blocks, 9; decorative, 64, *67*

Arch, brick: buck for, 112, *113-114;* constructing, *113-116;* elliptical, 112, *117;* factory-cut bricks for, 112; jack, 112, *118-121;* pointed, 112, *118;* segmental, 112, *117;* semicircular, 112, *113-116;* structure of, *112*

Arch, stone: buck for, *122, 123, 124;* building, *122-125;* mortar for, 122; semicircle, *124-125;* sloping, *122-124;* stones for, *122*

Backhoe, excavating with, 34, *36*

Baffles, for stepped footing, 40, *44*

Basalt, properties of, 11

Batter boards: *horizontal corner boards, mounted on stakes, that support strings for building lines and act as reference points.* In excavating, 34, *36;* setting up, 28, *29-30, 32*

Bituminous coating: *a coal-tar or asphalt coating painted onto block or concrete walls to waterproof the wall below ground.* Applying, 62, *63*

Blockouts: *foam or wood forms that prevent concrete from flowing into areas of a wall.* Bulkhead, *59;* using, 52, *57-58*

Bonds: common, 99; English, 99; Flemish, *99-100*

Brick(s): bricklaying techniques, 98, *99-100, 101;* building, 8; cleaning old, 23; cored, 8; decorative bonds, *99-100;* dismantling a wall, 22, 23; face, 8; fasteners for, *20-21;* frogged, 8; grades of, 8; ordering, 8-9; size of, 8, 51; special shapes, 8; standardization, 51; testing for water absorption, 9; water-table, 8. *See also* Arch, brick; Wall, brick

Brick veneer, 84, *85-89;* over concrete block, 89; estimating quantity of bricks, 84; finishing, 88; laying bricks, *86-88;* lintels, 84, *87-88;* marking courses, *85;* rowlock sill, *89;* veneering an existing structure, 84, *85;* wall ties,

84, *87;* weep holes, 85, *87, 88*

Buck: *temporary support used in constructing an arch.* For brick arch, 112, *113-114;* for stone arch, *122, 123, 124*

Building codes, specifications of, 27

Building inspection, applying for, 52

Building lines: laying out, *28-32;* liming, *31;* for stepped footing, *33;* using a transit level, *32-33*

Bulldozer, for grading, 34

Cinder blocks, 9

Concrete: air-entrained, for footings, 40; breaking up a slab, 22; cutting and drilling, *16-19;* fasteners for, *20-21;* pouring, 60, *61. See also* Footing; Slab foundation; Wall, poured-concrete

Concrete blocks: aggregate in, 9; bullnose, 9; corner, 9; faceted, 9; sizes, 9; speed blocks, 9; stretcher, 9; uses, 9; veneering with brick, 89. *See also* Retaining walls; Wall, concrete-block

Concrete blocks, casting: coloring, 64; decorative aggregates, 64, *67;* mass-producing, 65; mixing concrete, 64; patterned and textured, 64, *66-67;* steppingstones formed in the earth, 65; wooden forms, 64, *65*

Corner leads: *stepped rows of bricks or blocks raised at the corners to keep courses of masonry straight and true.* In concrete-block wall, 73, *75-76*

Cove: *sealed joint between walls and footings of foundation.* Waterproofing the wall, 62

Curve, cutting in stone, *14*

Cutting and drilling: with abrasive saw, 16, *19;* with hammer drill, 16, *17;* with rotary hammer, 16, *18;* with star drill, 16

Demolition: breaking up a slab, *22;* pulling down a brick wall, 23; using a jackhammer, 22

Drainage: in concrete slab, *46-47;* and retaining walls, 94, *97*

Dry-shake: *powdered mixture for coloring concrete.* Applying, 64

Excavating, *34-39;* with machines, 34, *36-37;* rough-grading, *35;* shoring, *38-39;* for slab, 46

Fasteners: expansion anchors, 20, *21;* installing, 20, *21;* masonry nails, 20, *21;* masonry screws, 20, *21;* steel pins, 20,

21; toggles, 20, *21*

Fieldstone: *unquarried stones found in fields.* Digging out, 10, *15*

Footing: for a brick wall, 98; for a concrete-block structure, *74, 75;* curved, 40, *42;* digging trench with power trencher, *37;* earth-formed, 41; foundation (poured-concrete), 40, *41-45;* keyed, 40, *45;* for latticework wall, *105;* pouring, *44-45;* reinforcing, 40, *42-43;* for retaining wall, 94; on sandy soil, 40; for serpentine wall, *108, 109;* for turned-down slab, 46; wood forms, *41-42;* stepped, *33,* 40, *43, 44, 45;* for stone wall, 90

Foundation wall: setting batter boards, *29-30, 32;* excavating, 34, *35-39;* laying out building lines, *28-32;* laying out site with transit level, *31-32;* poured-concrete footings, 40, *41-45;* poured-concrete walls, 52, *53-61;* shoring, *38-39;* slab, *46-50;* stepped footing, *33;* waterproofing, *62-63*

Frost line, 27, 40, 94, 98, 108

Grade beams: *footing reinforcements for a turned-down slab.* Installing, 46, *50*

Grade pegs: *rebar set in footing to indicate footing height.* In foundation footing, 40, *41*

Grading terrain, 34, *35*

Granite, 10; properties of, 11

Jack arch: building, *118-121;* lintel for, 112, *119, 120;* ordering bricks, 118

Jackhammer, *22*

Latticework wall: building with bricks, 98, *105-107;* capping, *107*

Limestone, 10; properties of, 11

Lintel: for jack arch, 112, *119, 120;* precast, for concrete-block structure, *74, 82;* supporting bricks in veneered wall, 84, *87-88*

Mortar: in brick wall, 98, *101;* grapevine joint, *101;* in joints between adobe bricks, 68; mixing, 74; for stone arch, 122; for stone wall, 90; tinting, 64; tooling, *101;* weeping joint, *101*

Muriatic acid, cleaning bricks with, *23*

Pier, reinforcing footing with rebar, *43*

Property line, locating, 28